YOUTH . . . and AGE

"It's true that physically we're strong and energetic, and that we dance and surf and ride around on motorbikes and stay up all night while the parents shake their heads and say, 'Oh, to be young again.' What sticks in my head, though, is another image. I hear low, barely audible speech, words breathed out as if by some supreme and nearly superhuman effort, I see limp gestures and sedentary figures. Kids sitting listening to music, sitting rapping, just sitting. Or sleeping—that most of all. Staying up late, but sleeping in later . . ."

Joyce Maynard

Looking Back

AVON
PUBLISHERS OF BARD, CAMELOT, DISCUS, EQUINOX AND FLARE BOOKS

Some of this material first appeared in the following periodicals:
New York Times Magazine, "An 18-Year-Old Looks Back on
Life"; *New York Times*, "No News from Cheshire High";
Mademoiselle, "The Embarrassment of Virginity"; *Seventeen*,
"Country Music", Copyright © 1971 by Triangle Communica-
tions, Inc.; *Newsweek*, "My Turn—Searching for Sages."

AVON BOOKS
A division of
The Hearst Corporation
959 Eighth Avenue
New York, New York 10019

First Avon Printing, March, 1974.

AVON TRADEMARK REG. U.S. PAT. OFF. AND
FOREIGN COUNTRIES, REGISTERED TRADEMARK—
MARCA REGISTRADA, HECHO EN CHICAGO, U.S.A.

Printed in the U.S.A.

To My Parents

Looking
Back

TO MY friend Hanna, at five, I am a grown-up. I do not feel like one—at nineteen, I'm at the midway point between the kindergartner and her mother, and I belong to neither generation—but I can vote, and drink in New York, and marry without parental consent in Mississippi, and get a life sentence, not reform school, if I shoot someone premeditatedly. Walking with Hanna in New York and keeping to the inside, as the guidebooks tell me, so that doorway muggers lunging out will get not her but me, I'm suddenly aware that, of the two of us, I am the adult, the one whose life means less, because I've lived more of it already; I've moved from my position as protected child to child protector; I am the holder of a smaller hand where, just ten years ago, *my* hand was held through streets whose danger lay not in the alleys but in the roads themselves, the speeding cars, roaring motorcycles. I have left childhood, and though I longed to leave it, when being young meant finishing your milk and missing "Twilight Zone" on TV because it came on too late, now that it's gone I'm uneasy. Not fear of death yet (I'm still young enough to feel immortal) or worry over wrinkles and gray

9

hair, but a sense that the fun is over before it began, that I'm old before my time—why isn't someone holding *my* hand still, protecting *me* from the dangers of the city, guiding me home?

I remember kneeling on the seat of a subway car, never bothering to count the stops or peer through all those shopping bags and knees to read the signs, because *she* would know when to get off, she'd take my hand; I remember looking out the window to see the sparks fly, underpants exposed to all the rush-hour travelers and never worrying that they could see, while all around me, mothers had to cross their legs or keep their knees together. And later, driving home, leaning against my mother's shoulder while her back tensed on the seat and her eyes stared out at the yellow lines, it was so nice to know I was responsible for nothing more than brushing my teeth when we got home, and not even that, if we got home late enough.

Hanna doesn't look where we're going, never bothers to make sure she can find her way home again, because she knows I will take care of those things, and though I feel I am too young to be so old in anybody's eyes, it's just a feeling, not a fact. When it rains, she gets the plastic rain hat, and when the ball of ice cream on her cone falls off, I give her mine. But if Hanna uses my ice cream and my hat, my knowledge of the subways and my hand, well, I use Hanna too: she's my excuse to ride the Ferris wheel, to shop for dolls. And when the circus comes to town—Ringling Brothers, no less—and I take her, everything evens up. Walking to Madison Square Garden, stepping over sidewalk lines and dodging muggers, she is my escort more than I am hers.

I think of one time in particular.

There we sat, in our too-well-cushioned seats, Hanna in her navy blue knee socks and flower barrettes, I beside her, holding the overpriced miniature flashlight she had shamed me into buying (because everyone else in our row had one), earnestly obeying the ringmaster's instructions to wave it when the lights went out—frantically, a beacon in the night—because Hanna's hands were too full of other circus-going apparatus: a celluloid doll whose arm already hung loose, the Cracker Jack she wanted for the prize inside, the Jujubes that she swallowed dutifully like pills. We all seemed a little sad, Hanna and me and all the other flashlight wavers who surrounded us, like people I'd see in a movie and feel sorry for—the grown-ups, the ticket buyers, because the admission fee hadn't really bought us into youngness again, even the little kids, because most of them had barely had it to begin with. We grew up old, Hanna even more than I. We are cynics who see the trap door in the magic show, the pillow stuffing in Salvation Army Santa Clauses, the camera tricks in TV commercials ("That isn't really a genie's hand coming out of the washing machine," Hanna tells me, "it's just an actor with gloves on.") So at the circus, there was a certain lack of wonder in the crowd, a calm, shrugging atmosphere of "So what else is new?" She leaned back on her padded seat, my four-year-old, watching me twirl her flashlight for her ("Keep up with those flashlights, kids," the ringmaster had said), chewing her hot dog, anticipating pratfalls, toughly, smartly, sadly, wisely, agedly unenthralled more wrapped up in the cotton candy than in the Greatest Show on Earth. Above us, a man danced on a tightrope while, below, poodles stood on their heads and elephants balanced, two-legged, over the spangled bodies of trusting circus girls, and horses leapt through flaming hoops and jugglers handled more balls than I could count and never dropped one.

Perhaps it was that we had too much to look at and so weren't awed by any one thing. But even more, it was that we had seen greater spectacles, unmoved, that our whole world was a visual glut, a ten-ring circus even Ringling Brothers couldn't compete with. A man stuck his head into a tiger's mouth and I pointed it out, with more amazement than I really felt, to my cool, unfazed friend, and when she failed to look (I, irritated now—"these seats cost money . . .") turned her head for her, forced her to take the sight in. The tiger could have bitten the tamer's head off, I think, swallowed him whole and turned into a monkey and she wouldn't have blinked. We watched what must have been two dozen clowns pile out of a Volkswagen without Hanna's knowing what the point of all that was. It isn't just the knowledge that they emerge from a trap door in the sawdust that keeps Hanna from

looking up, either. Even if she didn't know the trick involved, she wouldn't care.

I don't think I'm reading too much into it when I say
that, at five, she has already developed a sense of the ab-
surd—the kind of unblinking world-weariness that usually
comes only to disillusioned middle-aged men and eighty-
year-old rocking-chair sitters. I sometimes forget that
Hanna is just five, not eighty; that she believes she will
grow up to be a ballerina and tells me that someday she'll
marry a prince; that she is afraid of the dark, she isn't big
enough for a two-wheeler; her face clouds over in the sad
parts of a Shirley Temple movie and lights up at the orange roof of a Howard Johnson's. Maybe I'm projecting
on Hanna the feelings I have about my own childhood and
growing up when I say that she seems, sometimes, to be
so jaded. I think not, though. I watch her watching the
monkeys dance and, sensing my eyes on her, and for my
benefit, not from real mirth, she laughs a TV-actress
laugh. She throws her head back (a shampoo ad) and
smiles a toothpaste commercial smile so that baby teeth
show—sex appeal?—and says, for my benefit, "This is lots
of fun, isn't it?" the way people who aren't enjoying themselves much, but feel they should be, try to convince themselves they are.

What all this has to do with growing up old—Hanna
and me, five and nineteen, watching the circus—is that
Hanna has already begun her aging and I, once having
aged, am trying to return. We're different generations, of
course, but—though Hanna doesn't know what Vietnam
is, or marijuana—we've both been touched by the sixties
or, at least, its aftermath. I've grown up old, and I mention Hanna because she seems to have been born that
way, almost, as if each generaton tarnishes the innocence
of the next. In 1957 I was four going on twenty, sometimes; Hanna at the circus borders on middle age ... I
feel the circle—childhood and senility—closing in.

A word like *disillusioned* doesn't apply to a five-year-
old's generation or—though they call my generation "disillusioned" all the time—to mine. I grew up without many
illusions to begin with, in a time when fairy tales were
thought to be unhealthy (one teacher told my mother
that), when fantasy existed mostly in the form of Mr.

Clean and Speedy Alka-Seltzer. We were sensible, realistic, literal-minded, unromantic, socially conscious and politically minded, whether we read the papers (whether we could even read, in fact) or not. The Kennedys were our fairy-tale heroes, integration and outer space and The Bomb the dramas of our first school years. It was not a time when we could separate our own lives from the outside world. The idea then was *not* to protect the children—"expose" them, that was the term, and surely there's some sense, at least, in that—but it was carried too far with us. We were dragged through the mud of Relevance and Grim Reality, and now we have a certain tough, I've-been-there attitude. Not that we really know it all, but we often think we do. Few things shock or surprise us, little jolts our stubborn sureness that our way is right or rattles our early formed and often ill-founded, opinionated conclusions. We imagine hypocrisy in a politician's speeches. We play at vulnerability—honesty, openness, the sensitivity-group concept of *trust*, but what we're truly closer to is venerability. I think of the sixteen-year-old McGovern worker who tells me she was an idealistic socialist when she was young, and of the whole new breed, just surfacing, of drug users who have come full circle and, at twenty, given up dope (before some of us have begun, even).

All of which adds to this aged, weary quality I'm talking about. Oh yes, I know we are the Pepsi Generation. I know what they all say about our "youthful exuberance"—our music, our clothes, our freedom and energy and go-power. And it's true that, physically, we're strong and energetic, and that we dance and surf and ride around on motorbikes and stay up all night while the parents shake their heads and say "Oh, to be young again . . ." What sticks in my head, though, is another image. I hear low, barely audible speech, words breathed out as if by some supreme and nearly superhuman effort, I see limp gestures and sedentary figures. Kids sitting listening to music, sitting rapping, just sitting. Or sleeping—that, most of all. Staying up late, but sleeping in later. We're tired, often more from boredom than exertion, old without being wise, worldly not from seeing the world but from watching it on television.

Every generation thinks it's special—my grandparents because they remember horses and buggies, my parents because of the Depression. The over-thirties are special because they knew the Red Scare and Korea, bobby socks and beatniks. My older sister is special because she belonged to the first generation of teen-agers (before that, people in their teens were *adolescents*), when being a teen-ager was still fun. And I am caught in the middle. Mine is the generation of unfulfilled expectations. "When you're older," my mother promised, "you can wear lipstick." But when the time came, of course, lipstick wasn't being worn. "When we're big, we'll dance like that," my friends and I whispered, watching Chubby Checker twist on "American Bandstand." But we inherited no dance steps; ours was a limp, formless shrug to watered-down music that rarely made the feet tap. "Just wait till we can vote," I said, bursting with ten-year-old fervor, ready to fast, freeze, march and die for peace and freedom as Joan Baez, barefoot, sang, "We Shall Overcome." Well, now we can vote, and we're old enough to attend rallies and knock on doors and wave placards, and suddenly it doesn't seem to matter any more. My generation is special because of what we missed rather than what we got, because in a certain sense we are the first and the last. The first to take technology for granted. (What was a space shot to us, except an hour cut from social studies to gather before a TV in the gym as Cape Canaveral counted down?) The first to grow up with TV. My sister was eight when we got our set, so to her it seemed magic and always somewhat foreign. She had known books already and would never really replace them. But for me, the TV set was like the kitchen sink and the telephone, a fact of life.

We inherited a previous generation's hand-me-downs and took in the seams, turned up the hems, to make our new fashions. We took drugs from the college kids and made them a high school commonplace. We got the Beatles, but not those lovable look-alikes in matching suits with barber cuts and songs that made you want to cry. They came to us like a bad joke—aged, bearded, discordant. And we inherited the Vietnam war just after the crest of the wave—too late to burn draft cards and too early not to be drafted. The boys of 1953—my year—will be the last to go.

So where are we now? Generalizing is dangerous. Call us the apathetic generation and we will become that. Say times are changing, nobody cares about prom queens and getting into the college of his choice any more—say that (because it sounds good, it indicates a trend, gives a symmetry to history) and you make a movement and a unit out of a generation unified only in its common fragmentation. We tend to stay in packs, of course—at rock concerts and protest marches, but not so much because we are a real group as because we are, for all our talk of "individuality" and "doing one's thing," conformists who break traditions, as a rule, only in the traditional ways.

Still, we haven't all emerged the same because our lives were lived in high school corridors and drive-in hamburger joints as well as in the pages of *Time* and *Life* and the images on the TV screen. National and personal memory blur so that, for me, November 22, 1963, was a birthday party that had to be called off and Armstrong's moon walk was my first full can of beer. But memory—shared or unique—is, I think, a clue to why we are where we are now. Like over-anxious patients in analysis, we treasure the traumas of our childhood. Ours was more traumatic than most. The Kennedy assassination had become our myth: talk to us for an evening or two—about movies or summer jobs or the weather—and the subject will come up ("where were *you* when you heard . . ."), as if having lived through Jackie and the red roses, John-John's salute and Oswald's on-camera murder justifies our disenchantment. If you want to know who we are now—if you wonder whether ten years from now we will end up just like all those other generations that thought they were special—with 2.2 kids and a house in Connecticut—if that's what you're wondering, look to the past because, whether we should blame it or not, we do.

Durham, New Hampshire, where I come from, is a small town. There are no stop lights or neon signs on Main Street. We used to have an ice-cube machine but the zoning board and the town grandfathers sent it away to someplace less concerned with Old New England charm—some place where cold drinks are more important than tourists in search of atmosphere. The ugliest part of town is a row of gas stations that cluster at the foot of Church Hill and the Historical Society's rummage sale museum. Supershell-wegivestampsmobiloilyoumayhavealreadywon . . . their banners blow in our unpolluted winds like a Flag Day line-up at the UN. Dropouts from Lyster River High man the pumps and the greasers who are still in school, the shop boys, screech into the stations at lunchtime to study their engines and puff on cigarettes and—if there's been an accident lately—to take a look at the wrecks parked out back. When the rivers melt for swimming, sixth-grade boys bike to the stations—no hands—to pump up their tires and collect old inner tubes. Eighth graders come in casual, blushing troups to check out the dispensers in the Shell station's men's room. Nobody stays at the gas stations for long. They rip out to the highway or down a dirt road that leads to the rapids or back to town where even the grocery store is wreathed in ivy.

Proud of our quaintness, we are self-conscious, as only a small New Hampshire town that is also a university town just on the edge of sophistication can be. The slow, stark New England accents are cultivated with the corn. We meet in the grocery store and shake our heads over changes—the tearing down of Mrs. Smart's house to make way for a parking lot; the telephone company's announcement that dialing four digits was no longer enough, we'd need all seven; the new diving board at the town pool. . . . Durham is growing. Strange babies eat sand in the wading water and the mothers gathered to watch them no longer know each other's names. The old guard—and I am one—feel almost resentful. What can they know, those army-base imports, those Boston commuters with the Illinois license plates, those new faculty members and supermarket owners who weren't around the year it snowed so hard we missed four days of school and had to make it up on Saturdays. . . .

Yet all the while I was growing up in this town, I itched to leave. In September I'd visit the city for school clothes and wish I lived there always. In Boston, where I could go shopping every day and never worry about shoveling snow or pulling weeds. I tried hard for sophistication—with my

Boston dresses and my New York magazines and my Manchester high-heeled boots. Now that I've left I've discovered my loyalties—I play the small-town girl and pine for a Thornton Wilder dream that never really existed, a sense of belonging, the feeling that I'm part of a community.

In truth, what I have always been is an outsider. Midnight on New Year's Eve I would be reading record jackets or discussing the pros and cons of pass-fail grading with an earnest, glasses-polishing scholar who spoke of "us" and "we" as if I were just like him, or cleaning up the floor and the clothes of some ninth-grade boy who hadn't learned yet that you don't gulp down scotch the way you gulp down Kool-Aid. Many paper cups of Bourbon past the point where others began to stumble and slur and put their arms around each other in moments of sudden kinship, I remained clear-headed, unable to acquire that lovely warm fog that would let me suspend judgment, sign "Love always" in yearbooks (thinking that I meant it), put down my pencil and just have a good time. But liquor seems almost to sharpen my quills, to set me farther apart.

Sometimes I pretend, but I can always hear, off in the distance, the clicking of a typewriter. I see myself in the third person, a character in a book, an actor in a movie. I don't say this proudly but as a confession that, even as a friend told me another friend had died the night before I felt not only shock and grief but someday-I'll-write-about-this. And here I am now, doing it.

It must seem, to people who don't know me and even more, perhaps, to the ones who do, as if I'm a cold-blooded traitor, informing on a world that trusted me enough to let me in. So let me say first off that, whatever I say about the Girl Scouts and the cheerleaders and the soccer players and the high school drama club, the person I'm informing on most of all is myself. I'm not writing nostalgically, so the memories may not come out the way some people would like to remember them. (Listen to a twelve-year-old, sometime, reminiscing about the good old days when she was eight. Unable to feel wholeness and happiness in the present, we fabricate happy memories.) I don't look back in anger, either; maybe it's Freudian psychology that has made us so suspicious of our pasts. Whatever the reason, there's an awful lot of bitterness around, too many excuses made, too much stuffed in closets and blamed on things beyond control—parents and wars and teachers and traumas that became real only after the event, when we learned what traumas were.

As for looking back, I do it reluctantly. Sentimentality or bitterness—it breeds one or the other almost inevitably. But the fact is that there's no understanding the future without the present, and no understanding where we are now without a glance, at least, to where we have been.

1962

I didn't know till years later that they called it the Cuban Missile Crisis. But I remember Castro. (We called him Castor Oil and were awed by his beard—beards were rare in those days.) We might not have worried so much (what would the Communists want with our small New Hampshire town?) except that we lived ten miles from an air base. Planes buzzed around us like mosquitoes that summer. People talked about fallout shelters in their basements and one family on our street packed their car to go to the mountains. I couldn't understand that. If everybody was going to die, I certainly didn't want to stick around, with my hair falling out and—later—a plague of thalidomide-type babies. I wanted to go quickly, with my family. Dying didn't bother me so much—I'd never known anyone who died, and death was unreal, fascinating. (I wanted Doctor Kildare to have more terminal cancer patients and fewer love affairs.) What bothered me was the business of immortality. Sometimes growing-up sorts of concepts germinate slowly, but the full impact of death hit me like a bomb in the night. Not only would my body be gone—that I could take—but I would cease to think. That

I would no longer be a participant I had realized before; now I saw that I wouldn't even be an observer. What specially alarmed me about The Bomb (always singular like, a few years later, the Pill) was the possibility of total obliteration. All traces of me would be destroyed. There would be no grave and, if there were, no one left to visit it. Newly philosophical, I pondered the universe. If the earth was in the solar system and the solar system was in the galaxy and the galaxy was in the universe, what was the universe in? And if the sun was just a dot—the head of a pin—what was I? We visited a planetarium that year, in third grade, and saw a dramatization of the sun exploding. Somehow the image of that orange ball zooming toward us merged with my image of The Bomb. The effect was devastating, and for the first time in my life—except for Easter Sundays, when I wished I went to church so I could have a fancy new dress like my Catholic and Protestant friends—I longed for religion.

OYSTER RIVER Elementary was not a good school. They told us constantly that it was one of the best in the state, but the state was New Hampshire, and that was like calling an ant hill the highest point around because it rose up from the Sahara Desert. One fact of New Hampshire politics I learned early: we had no broad base tax. No sales or income tax because the antifederalist farmers and shoe factory workers who feared the Reds and creeping socialism acquired their political philosophy from William Loeb's Manchester *Union Leader* (the paper that, on the day of Joe McCarthy's death, ran his full page photo edged in black). We in Durham were a specially hated target, a pocket of liberals filling the minds of New Hampshire's young with highfalutin intellectual garbage. And that was why the archaic New Hampshire legislature always cut the university budget in half, and why my family had only one car, second hand (my father taught at the university). And the *Union Leader* was the reason, finally, why any man who wanted to be elected governor had first to pledge himself against the sales tax, so schools were supported by local property taxes and the

21

sweepstakes, which meant that they weren't supported very well. So Oyster River was not a very good school.

But in all the bleakness—the senile teacher who fell asleep at her desk; the annual memorization of Kilmer's *Trees*, the punishment administered by banging guilty heads on hard oak desks—we had one fine, fancy new gimmick that followed us from fourth grade through eighth. It was a box of white cardboard folders, condensed two-page stories about dinosaurs and earthquakes and Seeing Eye dogs, with questions at the end. The folders were called Power Builders and they were leveled according to color—red, blue, yellow, orange, brown—all the way up to the dreamed-for, cheated-for purple. Power Builders came with their own answer keys, the idea being that you moved at your own rate and—we heard it a hundred times—that when you cheat, you only cheat yourself. The whole program was called SRA and there were a dozen other abbreviations, TTUM, FSU, PQB—all having to do with formulae that had reduced reading to a science. We had Listening Skill Builders too—more readers' digested mini-modules of information, read aloud to us while we sat, poised stiffly in our chairs, trying frantically to remember the five steps (SRQPT? VWCNB? XUSLN?) to Better Listening Comprehension. A Listening Skill Test would come later to catch the mental wanderers, the doodlers, the deaf.

I—and most of the others in the Purple group—solved the problem by tucking an answer key into my Power Builder and writing down the answers (making an occasional error for credibility) without reading the story or the questions. By sixth grade a whole group of us had been promoted to a special reading group and sent to an independent study conference unit (nothing was a *room* any more) where we copied answer keys, five at a time, and then told dirty jokes.

SRA took over reading the way New Math took over arithmetic. By seventh grade there was a special Developmental Reading class. (Mental reading we called it.) The classroom was filled with audio-visual aids, phonetics charts, reading laboratories. Once a week the teacher plugged in the speed-reading machine that projected a story on the board, one phrase at a time, faster and faster. Get a piece of dust in your eye, blink—and you were lost.

There were no books in the Developmental Reading room—the lab. Even in English class we escaped books easily. The project of the year was to portray a famous author (one of the one hundred greatest of all time). I was Louisa May Alcott and my best friend was Robert McCloskey, the man who wrote *Make Way for Ducklings*. For this, we put on skits, cut out pictures from magazines and—at the end of the year, dressed up. (I wore a long nightgown with my hair in a bun and got A-plus; my friend came as a duck.) I have never read a book by Louisa May Alcott. I don't think I read a book all that year. All through high school, in fact, I barely read. Though I've started reading now in college, I still find myself drawn in bookstores to the bright covers and shiny, Power-Builder look. My eyes have been trained to skip nonessentials (adjectives, adverbs) and dart straight to the meaty phrases. (TVPQM.) But—perhaps in defiance of that whirring black rate-builder projector—it takes me three hours to read one hundred pages.

I watch them every year, the six-year-olds, buying lunch boxes and snap-on bow ties and jeweled barrettes, swinging on their mothers' arms as they approach the school on registration day or walking ahead a little, stiff in new clothes. Putting their feet on the shoe salesman's metal foot measurer, eying the patent leather and ending up with sturdy brown tie oxfords, sitting rigid in the barber's chair, heads balanced on white-sheeted bodies like cherries on cupcakes, as the barber snips away the kindergarten hair for the new grown-up cut, striding past the five-year-olds with looks of knowing pity (ah, youth) they enter elementary school, feigning reluctance—with scuffing heels and dying TV cowboy groans shared in the cloakroom, but filled with hope and anticipation of all the mysteries waiting in the cafeteria and the water fountain and the paper closet, and in the pages of the textbooks on the teachers' desks. With pink erasers and a sheath of sharpened pencils, they file in so really bravely, as if to tame lions, or at least subdue the alphabet. And instead, I long to warn them, watching this green young crop pass by each year,

seeing them enter a red-brick, smelly-staircase world of
bathroom passes and penmanship drills, gongs and red
x's, and an unexpected snap to the teacher's slingshot
voice (so slack and giving, when she met the mothers). I
want to tell them about the back pages in the teacher's
record book, of going to the principal's office or staying
behind an extra year. Quickly they learn how little use
they'll have for lion-taming apparatus. They are, themselves, about to meet the tamer.

I can barely remember it now, but I know that I once
felt that first-day eagerness too. Something happened,
though, between that one pony-tail-tossing, skirt-flouncing,
hand-waving ("*I* know the answer—call on *me*") day and
the first day of all the other years I spent in public school.
It wasn't just homework and the struggle to get up at
seven every morning, it was the *kind* of homework assign-
ments we were given and the prospect of just what it was
that we were rousing ourselves for—the systematic breaking down, workbook page by workbook page, drill after
drill, of all the joy we started out with. I don't think I'm
exaggerating when I say that, with very few exceptions,
what they did to (not *for*) us in elementary school was
not unlike what I would sometimes do to my cats: dress
them up in doll clothes because they looked cute that way.

We were forever being organized into activities that, I
suspect, looked good on paper and in school board reports. New programs took over and disappeared as ap-
proaches to child education changed. One year we would
go without marks, on the theory that marks were a "poor
motivating factor," "an unnatural pressure," and my labo-
riously researched science and social studies reports would
come back with a check mark or a check plus inside the
margin. Another year every activity became a competition, with posters tacked up on the walls showing who was
ahead that week, our failures and our glories bared to all
the class. Our days were filled with electrical gimmicks,
film strips and movies and overhead projectors and tapes
and supplementary TV shows, and in junior high, when we
went audio-visual, a power failure would have been reason
enough to close down the school.

But though the educational jargon changed, the school's
basic attitude remained constant. Anything too different

(too bad or too exceptional), anything that meant making another column in the record book, was frowned upon. A lone recorder, in a field of squeaking flutophones, a reader of Dickens, while the class was laboring page by page (out loud, pace set by the slowest oral readers) with the adventures of the Marshall family and their dog Ranger, a ten-page story when the teacher had asked for a two-pager—they all met with suspicion. Getting straight A's was fine with the school as long as one pursued the steady, earnest, unspectacular course. But to complete a piece of work well, without having followed the prescribed steps—that seemed a threat to the school, proof that we could progress without it. Vanity rears its head everywhere, even in the classroom, but surely extra guards against it should be put up there. I remember an English teacher who wouldn't grant me an A until second term, an indication, for whoever cared about that sort of thing, that under her tutelage I had *improved*. Every composition was supposed to have evolved from three progressively refined rough drafts. I moved in just the opposite direction for the school's benefit: I wrote my "final drafts" the first time around, then deliberately aged them a bit with earnest-looking smudges and erasures.

Kids who have gone through elementary school at the bottom of their class might argue here that it *was* the smart ones who got special attention—independent study groups, free time to spend acting in plays and writing novels (we were always starting autobiographies) and re-searching "Special Reports"—all the things that kept our groups self-perpetuating, with the children lucky enough to start out on top forever in the teacher's good graces, and those who didn't start there always drilling on decimals and workbook extra-work pages. But Oyster River was an exemplary democratic school and showed exemplary concern for slow students—the under-achievers—and virtuously left the quick and bright to swim for themselves, or tread water endlessly.

It always seemed to me as a Group One member, that there was little individual chance to shine. It was as if the school had just discovered the division of labor concept, and oh, how we divided it. Book reports, math problems, maps for history and even art projects—we did them all in committee. Once we were supposed to write a short story that way, pooling our resources of Descriptive Adjectives and Figures of Speech to come up with an adventure that read like one of those typing-book sentences ("A quick brown fox . . ."), where every letter of the alphabet is represented. Our group drawings had the look of movie magazine composites that show the ideal star, with Paul Newman's eyes, Brando's lips, Steve McQueen's hair. Most people loved group work—the kids because working together meant not working very hard, tossing your penny in the till and leaving it for someone else to count, the teachers because committee projects prepared us for community work, (getting along with the group, leadership abilities . . .) and, more important, I think, to some of them, they required a lot less marking time than individual projects did. The finished product didn't matter so much—in fact, anything too unusual seemed only to rock our jointly rowed canoe.

The school day was for me, and for most of us, I think, a mixture of humiliation and boredom. Teachers would use their students for the entertainment of the class. Within the first few days of the new term, someone quickly becomes the class jester, someone is the class genius, the "brain" who, the teacher, with doubtful modesty, reminds us often, probably has a much higher IQ than she. Some student is the trouble-maker black sheep (the one who always makes her sigh), the one who will be singled out as the culprit when the whole class seems like a stock exchange of note passing, while all the others stare at him, looking shocked.

Although their existence is denied now, in this modern, psychologically enlightened age, teachers' pets are still very much around, sometimes in the form of the girl with super-neat penmanship and Breck-clean hair, sometimes in the person of the dependable Brain, who always gets called on when the superintendent is visiting the class. Teachers, I came to see, could be intimidated by a class, coerced or conned into liking the students who were popular among the kids, and it was hard not to miss, too, that many teachers were not above using unpopular students to gain acceptance with the majority. They had an instinct, teachers did, for who was well-liked and who wasn't; they learned all the right nicknames and turned away, when they could, if one of their favorites was doing the kind of thing that brought a 3 in conduct. We saw it all, like underlings watching the graft operations of ambitious politicians, powerless to do anything about it.

That was what made us most vulnerable: our powerlessness. Kids don't generally speak up or argue their case. No one is a child long enough, I suppose, or articulate enough, while he is one, to become a spokesman for his very real, and often oppressed, minority group. And then when we outgrow childhood, we no longer care, and feel, in fact, that if *we* went through it all, so should the next generation. Children are *expected* to be adversaries of school and teachers, so often, in the choosing up of sides, parents will side with the school. Nobody expects children to like school; therefore it's no surprise when they don't. What should be a surprise is that they dislike it for many good reasons.

It would be inaccurate to say I hated school. I had a good time sometimes, usually when I was liked, and therefore on top. And with all the other clean-haired girls who had neat penmanship and did their homework, I took advantage of my situation. When I was on the other side of the teacher's favor though, I realized that my sun-basking days had always depended on there being someone in the shade. That was the system—climbing up on one another's heads, putting someone down so one's own stature could be elevated. Elementary school was a club that not only reinforced the class system but created it—a system in which the stutterer and the boy who can't hit a baseball start out, and remain, right at the bottom, a system where being in the middle—not too high or low—is best of all.

I had imagined, innocently, on my first day of school, that once the kids saw how smart I was, they'd all be my friends. I see similar hopes on the faces I watch heading to the front every September—all the loved children, tops in their parents' eyes, off to be "re-evaluated" in a world where only one of thirty can be favorite, each child unaware, still, that he is not the only person in the universe, and about to discover that the best means of survival is to blend in (adapting to the group, it's called), to go from being one to being one in a crowd of many, many others.

1963

Fourth grade was the year of rationality, the calm before the storm. Boys still had cooties and dolls still tempted us. That was the year when I got my first Barbie. Perhaps they were produced earlier, but they didn't reach New Hampshire till late that fall, and the stores were always sold out. So at the close of our doll-playing careers there was a sudden dramatic switch in scale from lumpy, round-bellied Betsy Wetsys and stiff-legged little-girl dolls to slim curvy Barbie, just eleven inches tall, with a huge, expensive wardrobe that included a filmy black negligee, and a mouth that made her look as if she'd just swallowed a lemon. Barbie wasn't just a toy, but a way of living that moved us suddenly from tea parties to dates with Ken at the soda shoppe. Our short careers with Barbie, before junior high sent her to the attic, built up our expectations for teen-age life before we had developed the sophistication to go along with them. Children today are accustomed to having a tantalizing youth culture all around them. (They play with Barbie in the nursery school.) For us, it broke like a cloudburst, without preparation. Caught in the deluge, we were torn—wanting to run for shelter but tempted, also, to sing in the rain.

WHEN we were in fifth grade, the girls in Mrs. Herrick's. class were called aside and told that we were going to see a very lovely movie just for us, all about growing up. They gave us invitations to take home for our mothers so they could see the movie too, but I, like almost everybody else, disposed of mine long before I reached home, unspeakably embarrassed (because I knew, of course, what was coming—they'd been showing this movie for years), and the last thing I wanted was to sit through it with my mother, to let her know I knew, to see her seeing me. The boys pestered us, of course, and wanted to know what was going on; they were to spend that hour playing basketball and figured we must be cooking up some kind of party for them. A few of the worldlier ones were silent and understanding-looking (they had older sisters, and knew something about the Trials of Being a Woman) and one or two said, "I bet it's about Kotex"— they didn't quite know what it was, but they knew there was some kind of machine in the girls' room and they saw the ads in magazines and everybody knew the story of Tom Callahan, who, when his mother sent him to buy paper plates and napkins, came back with the wrong kind and said, "Feminine napkins, masculine napkins—what difference does it make?"

Some of the girls took all the questions from the boys in stride and said, "Get lost," or "Go blow." I wasn't really shy, and not a blusher, certainly, but this seemed too sensitive an area for casualness. Telling dirty jokes was one thing, but taking sex seriously (and not, as we usually did, giggling over its ickyness and groaning "Grossness *plus*")—that was harder. Four-letter words and slang I could pronounce with no trouble, but the official terms, the ones printed in the little pink booklet they gave us to take home, in preparation for the *Now That You're a Woman* film, words like that (and *woman* was one) caught in my throat. Becky and Carol and I looked in the dictionary for "menstruate" and "penis." Not for definitions, just to see the unspeakable in print. *The Old Man and the Sea* shocked and thrilled us because Hemingway had written for all to see—even teachers—*urinate*. (Worse still, he spoke of urinating over the side of a boat. "OOOhooh," we giggled, making faces, "*gro*-oos.")

The school nurse came to our classroom the day of the big movie to guide us through The Experience and answer questions afterward. (Who on earth would want or dare to ask a question?) A few mothers came too, and sat beside their daughters, who tried hard to ignore them. Our mothers, that year, were in the category of our going to the bathroom. Everybody knew we *did* (just as they knew we had mothers) but we tried to disavow any knowledge of those facts whenever possible. (That year I gave up drinking water during school because asking the teacher for a bathroom pass seemed just about unthinkable. That long walk up to her desk, with all eyes on me. Then down the hall and into the pink ammonia-smelling room marked Girls, with dirty pictures—done by girls, I wondered, or by infiltrating boys, and if they'd come in once, why not again?—and then those little cubicles with the doors that rarely stayed shut, unless you held them closed with your foot or went with a friend to stand guard, who'd hear you, then, and know that, just like everybody else, you *did it* too. Finally, to enter the classroom again, seeing everyone—especially the boys—look up. Knowing where you'd been, having imagined you there, most likely—just as, when they went, you imagine them, step by step, and tried to guess exactly when they'd reappear. Now he's flushing the toilet . . . now he's zipping up his fly . . . now he's washing up—or *did* boys wash?—and, if not—My *God*, you'd held their hands in gym class, doing foxtrot.)

Mrs. Logan, the nurse who came to speak to our class, was the same one who delivered me when I was born (an additional shame—she'd seen me naked). She introduced the film and talked very softly, as if someone had just died, about "something very beautiful and exciting" that was going to happen in our bodies. Then she turned out the lights. It was an animated film made by Walt Disney, with characters who had familiar Cinderella lips and Bambi eyes. But this time Disney was animating ovaries and uteruses, cute little eggs and wiggly sperm that looked like tadpoles. Worse than anything else about the whole humiliating event (it seemed so public, with nothing left to private discovery) was the fact that the film was made by Disney, joy of my childhood, who now escorted me out from the gilded carriage to be met by sperm-faced ushers at the door of this unpleasant new pumpkin.

Clearly not all the girls felt as I did. Some were full of questions when the movie finished, many of them the show-offy, asked-for-the-sake-of-asking kinds of questions whose answers could be of interest only to the asker, and probably not even to her. (Like the kids who, as late as twelfth grade, would hold up college boards by asking, "What do I put in the blank where it says 'middle name'—I don't have one.") My sense of delicacy about the subject was certainly extreme. But it seems to me, even now, unfair to put some kinds of young girls through the type of cheery, gung-ho, isn't-this-fun facts of life talk that they gave us at school. It wasn't the facts I objected to—sex education I certainly applaud. It was words like "special" and "cherish" and "miracle" and "gift," the notion of Woman's Secret Burden, with connotations of brave, silent suffering (the boys would never know what we went through—for them; we'd let them think they were the tough ones)—that's what I detested, and why I entered adolescence with some amount of anguish. The boys were almost encouraged to be goofy and playful,

happy-go-lucky, while we got left with being Woman, suddenly matronly, with images of cramps and making up excuses not to swim—all that ahead of us, our sexuality
something to be concealed, while boys could flaunt theirs
on their chests and chins. (They brandished their razors,
we hid ours.) I knew a girl whose mother said she
couldn't shave her legs till she was fourteen—while, at
twelve, she badly needed to, and had to pluck her legs,
like eyebrows, in a closet.

And then there were bras, and the dilemma—when to
buy one, what kind, when to wear it and with Kleenex
stuffed inside or not. Some girls really needed them by
junior high, and a few needed, but didn't wear them, and
came to crossing their arms or bundling up in thick cardi-
gans even in June. Others who didn't need bras wore them
anyway—flat strips of nylon stretched across flat chests,
worn for the telltale outline they made under jerseys, not
so much in the front, but in the back, and for those occa-
sions during dances when a boy would rub his hand across
your back and feel delicious pity at what you went
through (Burden of Womanhood again), all of which
made you, in your slavery, wonderfully feminine and—key
word—*vulnerable*. By our day, the bra had come full circle, from object of necessity to be concealed as best one
could to unnecessary object of fashion to be displayed,
where, as with make-up the idea was to let people know
you were wearing it, but just barely—making it look as if
you really didn't want people to see.

All fifth graders are obsessed with sex—the boys, with
their mostly bathroom and bosom humor, of course,
and—a bit more secretly, but more profoundly, the girls.
Never so loud or raucous, they do not leer or whistle, or
jab each other in the ribs and call out "I see London . . ."
when the waistband of a boy's shorts shows. Their sex talk
is softer because it's less taken for granted and smiled at
than the boys' is ("Boys will be boys . . ."), but it's there,
all right, whispered under the blankets at Girl Scout
sleepovers or in heads-together huddles on the playground.
Boys, coming home from school at three, would weave
and spin on their bikes, making little orbits around us as
we walked, standing up on the seats when they passed us,

to call out some new and thrilling combination of four-letter words, or taking their hands off the bars and giving us the finger. And we would clutch our neatly lettered notebooks to what we still shyly referred to as our "fronts" and speculate about the sex lives of our teachers. The little boys were being nothing more than little boys while we, the fifth-grade girls, who saw special movies and wore bras and dreamed of John Lennon and the eighth-grade baseball team, we were the true pornographers. Our shyness about real-life sex, when it concerned us personally, was concealed behind the gusto with which we dwelt upon its aberrations. Never acknowledging our own sexual vulnerability, we were thrilled, shocked and titillated by the exploits of others.

And in a classroom full of smart, wise-cracking dirty jokesters, I was the biggest know-it-all of all. Whether my sex information was accurate or not, the point is that I *thought* it was and, thinking that, I set myself up as the counselor and information center for our class. I was full of sex lore; I glibly expounded on the meanings of the most sophisticated *Playboy* jokes; I had vague but elaborate notions about lesbians and eunuchs and—when the explanations were too embarrassing to give—I escorted my friends into the girls' room at school, wrote out the definitions on toilet paper (or drew explanatory diagrams) then, after showing what I'd written, dramatically flushed them down the toilet. I wrote pornographic stories and circulated them at school, hoping of course, to buy myself an in. The situation is a common one: the never-wholly-accepted kid discovers that he's got something negotiable—a swimming pool, a talent for math, an electric Yo-yo, an exploitable knack for writing dirty stories and so he thinks, just briefly, that he can parlay what he has into social capital, that *now* he will be liked, plummeted to stardom. Cocker-spaniel eager, he repeats over and over the song and dance that worked so well, brought him such favor, the first time round. It's the one tune he knows, though, and so of course his audience tires of it— by that time, they've found a new court jester. The whole point of the jester system is that the briefly well-loved clown-show-off can gain at best only a temporary place within the group. He interests them only so long as he is

different from them. They are amused and entertained—
fond, even—because he is and will always remain an outsider.

Anyway, for a while I basked in my role as classroom
sex expert, until the subject filled my life almost completely. Somewhere I had read about phallic symbols, and
from then on my girl friends and I imagined them ev-
eryplace we looked, which wasn't hard, since everything
except a square is either longer than it is wide or wider
than it is long. (I realize this now, but back in fifth grade
it seemed as if my landscape was filled with innuendo,
with richly sexual, symbolic Meaning.) We marveled at
our history teacher's calm (how thick she was; didn't she
know?) as she described to us, while we sat frozen with
mixed relish and horror, that monumental event of 1889,
the erection of the Eiffel Tower.

I set myself up as a counselor too, full of advice for
girls just starting out with boy friends while I had none,
myself. Suddenly, though, just about everyone else knew
more than me, and what they knew came from experience, not books read in the closet, men's magazine advice
columns read, one sentence at a time, from quick, nervous
perusal in the drugstore. By seventh grade, the make-out
parties had begun, and my ribaldry wasn't funny any more
because it ridiculed a world more and more kids were en-
tering, while I remained outside.

MORE than anything else, I enjoy an experience that lets me like, really *like*, people. That's not so simple for me, quick to find fault and suspicious, when I don't find it, of over-goodness. It's not that I don't feel affection for a good many people, but blanket love, the kind Miss America contestants always swear to ("I love tennis and horseback riding and people . . .") has never come readily to me. That's what I liked about Pete Seeger—he brought out my most tolerant side. By all sorts of short-cut devices (a specially joyful banjo-picking style, blue lights, and certain combinations of notes—there must be a formula— that never fail to make me want to cry with love), somehow he always made me feel generous-spirited. It never worked on records, and two hours after hearing him, the desire to run away and join the Peace Corps or send my money to India would have worn off. But in the concert hall it worked. For once I didn't care about standing out—I reveled in assimilation. Boundaries (me and them) disappeared. It was *us*, the audience—we were a single body.

Pete Seeger didn't sing or play all that well. Often he

just strummed his guitar. Fancy picking wouldn't have seemed right for his gritty dust-bowl singing, his drab shirts and baggy pants that looked as if he'd spent the day farming. His Adam's apple was more memorable than his nose or his mouth—it throbbed, and seemed to be the heart of him. Resonant, mellow notes wouldn't have been right for that thin neck, stretched forward and turned toward the ceiling in a way that always made me think of a crowing rooster. His songs were not exactly distinguished either—rarely beautiful or sweet-sounding, anyway. They were simple lines you could sing along with and whistle later to yourself on the way home. Pete Seeger talked a lot during concerts. That was part of what you paid to get, the long, low-key introductions that explained what he was going to sing, or who wrote it. Not funny, Las Vegas-type jokes, these were more like bedtime stories, ramblings, and you were never quite sure when they were finished because they didn't have what you could call punch lines, or even endings.

But because nothing was so exquisitely beautiful you didn't dare touch it, it was fine to cough or sneeze during songs, if you needed to, or hum along, or clap in time, or sing as loud and off-key as you wanted. Pete Seeger taught us harmony parts and led sopranos, altos, tenors and bass all at once, switching melody lines from rooster-falsetto—with the neck stretched like a licorice whip—to low, low bass notes, losing the tune sometimes. He would cue us with each line just before we sang it, walking around the stage or putting his foot on a chair and stamping hard, turning red in the face and looking really happy, making us feel that we were a special audience, able still, after all these performances, to stir him on the final chorus of "Michael—Row the Boat Ashore." Then there was "Guantanamera," whose preface-story we all knew so well that he had only to say the first words for us to break into applause.

We sang "We Shall Overcome" and dedicated it to the civil rights workers who died in Mississippi, and once (I heard him often) he asked us all to take each other's hands so we formed a single chain. We sang "This Land Is Your Land," and I felt more patriotic than "America the Beautiful" at basketball games ever made me feel. We ap-

plauded ourselves at the end, and stood up, wishing there
was something more we could do than give a standing
ovation. Right then, with " ... this land is made for you
and me" still fresh and swirling, not yet settled in my
head, I would have jumped over the balcony or set fire to
my treasured purple concertgoing coat, I think, if he'd
asked me to.

I was eight when Joan Baez entered our lives, with long
black beatnik hair and a dress made out of a burlap bag.
When we got her first record (we called her Joan *Baze*
then—soon she was simply Joan) we listened all day, to
"All My Trials" and "Silver Dagger" and "Wildwood
Flower." My sister grew her hair and started wearing san-
dals, making pilgrimages to Harvard Square. I took up the
guitar. We loved her voice and her songs but, even more,
we loved the idea of Joan, like the fifteenth-century Girl
of Orléans, burning at society's stake, marching alone or
singing, solitary, in a prison cell to protest segregation. She
was the champion of nonconformity and so—like thou-
sands of others—we joined the masses of her fans . . .

Somehow I could never imagine Jackie Kennedy going to
the bathroom. I knew she must but she was too cool and
poised and perfect. We had a book about her, filled with
color pictures of Jackie painting in a spotless yellow linen
dress, Jackie on the beach with Caroline and John-John,
Jackie riding elephants in India and Jackie, in a long white
gown, greeting Khrushchev like Snow White welcoming
one of the seven dwarfs. (No, I wasn't betraying Joan in
my adoration. Joan was beautiful but human, like us;
Jackie was magic.) When, years later, she married
Rumpelstiltskin, I felt like a child discovering, in his father's drawer, the Santa Claus suit. And, later still, reading
some *Ladies' Home Journal* exposé ("Jacqueline Onassis'
secretary tells all . . .") I felt almost sick. After the first
few pages I put the magazine down. I wasn't interested in
the fragments, only in the fact that the glass had
broken . . .

I can remember—just barely—a time when I didn't know
who the Beatles were. People my age are about the last

generation who can say that—for the ones who were nine
or ten instead of twelve when the Beatles burst into our
consciousness, it must seem as if they have always been a
part of life. We were in fifth grade when they first sang on
the Ed Sullivan show to an audience that screamed so
loud we scarcely heard them. I had no desire to scream or
cry or throw jelly beans; an eighth grader would have
been old enough to revert to childhood, but I was too
young to act anything but old. Still, I remember that wonderful, shivery moment when I first experienced "I wanna
hold your hand," and it seemed as if a new color had been
invented.

Because I can remember life without the Beatles and
because it seems we aged together, I feel proprietary
about them, when I see the new young crop of fans
playing those first albums or, worse, abandoning them for
weaker imitations. I feel a little weary too; how could I
begin to explain what we've been through, John and Paul
and Ringo and George and I: Liverpool accents and "A
Hard Day's Night" and Cynthia and Jane Asher and a
reporter asking "What do you call your haircut?" and
George saying "Arthur" and Maharishi Mahesh Yogi and
Ravi Shankar and *Yellow Submarine* and things not sounding as pretty as they used to, and Yoko—like a bad taste
in the mouth—and Paul leaving and suing, and breaking
up finally, which freed us to love them again, as the death
of a senile grandparent frees the good memories.

The Beatles gave us something more than music. Quite
a lot, I think. For one thing, they made kids part of history—journalistic history, at any rate. Through the Beatles' existence we held some sort of control, we could act.
Their appearance gave us our first sense of youth as a
power—one that could hold moratoriums and keep LBJ
from seeking re-election and raise a couple of million dollars for Bangladesh, without depending on grown-ups for
anything. For that—for the fame they gave us—we gave
fame back to them.

My love for the Beatles at ten or eleven was, I think, a
pure, pre-teen-age love. They made me dream of dancing
and romance, of holding hands and sipping milkshakes together, riding on merry-go-rounds, images used on TV to
show that two people were in love. But it was never the

Beatles themselves that I imagined myself holding hands
with, although some girls did—they bought Beatle posters
and lunch boxes and sweatshirts and planned pilgrimages
to Liverpool, and abandoned them all a few months later
for the Dave Clark Five or the Beach Boys. I was too
practical for that. It seemed like a waste of time to swoon
over John when my chances of meeting him were so
slight, and anyway, he was already married.

The Rolling Stones were a different matter. No
matching collarless suits and hair like well-clipped shrub-
bery. They didn't want to hold your hand, they wanted
"Satisfaction," "girly action," "gang the groover" (I didn't
know quite what that meant, but something in the way the
Stones moved, the way they breathed and the way Mick
Jagger's eyes looked—damp and muddy—made me feel
funny). With the Beatles I felt a part of things; the Stones
made me feel hopelessly out of it. Clearly their league was
way beyond mine. I didn't hate them for it though. It was
a blissful pain—my age, and Mick Jagger's contempt for
it; the sinister look on Charlie Watts's face—just barely
grinning, as if he was imagining Ed Sullivan in his underwear, while they shook hands and Ed said "nice work,
boys" (these, obviously, were *men*); Mick's skinny hips
and his chicken-strutting (while the Beatles bounced in
place, more like the happy winners on quiz shows); Keith
Richard's ex-convict face. I imagined tough-looking girl
friends smoking backstage, with dyed red hair and tattoos,
chains and boots.

THE pressure of The Group is strong in any period. There was a new kind of pressure affecting us during the sixties though—not just the push toward conformity and the fear and distrust that people have by nature (and that public schools seem to reinforce) of anything that's different. In the fifties, I think, groups pretty rigidly conformed, but they were indiscriminating too. A pair of bobby sox, a V-necked sweater, and you were *in*. The sixties were a more critical-minded, sophisticated time, full of more negative adjectives than lavish superlatives, a time when it was easier to do things wrong than to do them right. Products, ourselves, of hours spent listening to TV commercials, we had become comparative shoppers, suspicious and demanding, minutely analyzing one another's actions and appearances—new haircuts with unevenly trimmed sideburns, cowlicks, unmatched socks, Band-Aids that, we suspected, concealed pimples, new dresses, new shoes. We knew each other's faces and bodies and wardrobes so well that any change was noticed at once, the fuel for endless notes. That's why I dressed so carefully mornings—I was about to face the scrutiny of fifteen gossip-seeking girls,

ten only slightly less observant boys ready to imitate my
voice and walk, and one stern, prune-faced teacher who
would check my spelling and my long division with the
care my enemies gave to my hems. At every moment—
even at home, with no one but family there—I'd be conscious of what the other kids, The Group, would think if
they could see me now.

They ruled over us all—and over each other—like a supreme court. Their presence was frightening, their judg-
ments quick and firm and often damning, and the tightness
of the circle when I was in it only made the times when I
was outside seem more miserable. The hierarchy was re-
established a hundred times a day—in choosing partners
for science experiments, in study halls, when the exchange
of homework problems began, and at lunch. But most of
all in note passing. We rarely needed to take notes, and so
we passed them. We could have whispered easily enough,
of course, or remained silent. (It wasn't ever that we had
important things to say.) But note passing was far more
intriguing, spylike. (Those were "The Man from
U.N.C.L.E." days, all of us playing Illya Kuryakin.) Most
of all, note passing was exclusive. Whispers were imper-
manent and could be overheard. Notes could be tightly
sealed and folded, their journeys followed down the rows
to make sure none was intercepted along the way. Getting
a note, even an angry one, was always a compliment.
Whenever I received one, I was amazed and grateful that
I had made some slight impression on the world, that I
was worthy of someone's time and ink. There were kids, I
knew, whose letters died, like anonymous fan mail, unan-
swered and unread.

I think it was in notes, more than in conversations or
Girl Scout meetings or Saturday mornings together on our
bikes, that friendships and hatreds were established. We
committed ourselves on paper to things we never would
have said out loud (this seems odd to me now) and we
saved them all—round-lettered, backhand messages written on blue-lined loose-leaf paper, the corners of old
workbook pages, candy wrappers, lunch bags; they circulated around the classroom from desk to desk and year to
year (once, in the seventh grade, we even had a pulley between desks). These were, I think, the greatest writing

practice we got in school. Sometimes the notes contained
news, stretched out in soap opera-type installment doses,
to last us through an uneventful day. Stories leaked
slowly—"Guess what?" would travel down my row to
Becky till, at last, the teacher's mind deep in another matter, my note would cross the hardest point along its
course, the latitudinal gulch between our rows (not within
them) and she would unwrap it, folded like an origami
bird, and write her answer, "What?" and pass it back to
me. We wrote about TV shows watched the night before,
about how much we hated math and what our weekend
and after-school plans were ("Are you going to walk
home or take the bus?" "Short cut or long way around?").

Great wars, or so they seemed to us, were waged in
notes, based on elaborate strategies we worked out, like
homework, the night before. If things were getting dull,
I'd plan to pick a fight, with accusations of two-facedness
(talking about someone behind his back was the most
common offense) or cruelty to an underdog. Realizing
early that I wasn't going to be a leader among the *in*, and
refusing to simply follow, I became the champion of the
class failures. The boy with the harelip, the girl who lived
in a trailer and smelled bad, the one who tended to drool
a little on her collar, I defended (enjoying the image of
myself as kind and gentle benefactress, protecting the sensitive, the poet soul) from the group I loved and envied—for their coolness—and hated for the fact that they
had never quite admitted me. I lectured Margie in suffering, histrionic moralistic tones ("You, who have always
been popular, cannot know what it's like not to be. Think,
for a moment, what Franny feels like when you laugh at
her or lead her on to make a fool of herself, because she
thinks that then you'll be her friend. I *know*—I know
what it's like on this side of the fence . . .") Margie, a genuinely friendly girl, would be first puzzled and defensive.
And then, as her troops moved in on me, sarcastic and
coldly vicious. She'd write back to deny the charges, and
there would be the ghastly period I always forgot about,
setting out on my battles, when I seemed to be sinking and
friendless, and wished I'd never started the whole thing.

Nothing felt worse than Margie's green eyes on you
when you were out of favor, waiting for you to reveal

weakness. When we were fighting, our lips set tight, and we walked in a special way, skirts swishing, tossing our hair behind our backs in a show of more confidence and contempt than we really felt. Margie's alliances were her advantage. Mine was my loner stance, the pretense I kept up of not caring, and the confidence I felt as a devastating note writer. (Inevitably, we got down to that—she scornful of the big words I used, I of her small ones. Our logic lacked much, but at the time I always felt like Perry Mason, pouncing down on her verbal inadequacies with what I saw as killing sarcasm. "It's clear from your spelling of 'deceive,' " I'd write, "that you are deceived yourself. Perhaps you need a dictionary." That, in seventh grade, seemed the height of cutting sophistication.) Finally the storm would break and we'd come to that lovely warm moment when, like the generals of warring armies meeting in no-man's land to make peace and shake hands, in separate and mutual admiration, we'd make up. First there would be long, honest outpourings from both sides, effusive apologies and confessions, secrets and much Honesty. Then she would smile at me and I would glow with the humble pride and gratitude that comes from understandings and alliances between adversaries. I loved those brief periods when we were friends.

Not until we graduated from high school and found ourselves, once out of competition, to be *friends*, did I discover that Margie, too—the coolest, most confident-looking golden girl of our class, whom I had always admired and envied, was herself less blithe than I'd imagined. We all have something of the observer in us, the detached outsider, the self-conscious partygoer who's capable of worrying, deep in a back-seat embrace, whether his/her breath smells of pizza, something of the grandstand football fan who's never quite sure, when the cheerleaders demand "Give us a *B*—" whether to give them one or not (looking around to see what the other kids—who may be looking at *him*—are doing). We are none of us quite as carefree as we look.

To be *popular*, like having a "good sense of humor" or "a great personality," has always seemed to me one of the doubtful virtues ascribed to cheerleaders in yearbooks. Although popularity is a word I've never warmed up to, I recognized the results of it every time we chose up teams in gym, every time there was a dance or a field trip. One could tell from where we sat in the lunchroom—the tables of girls with too-long dresses and hair that curled in the bent, squared-off way that came from using bobby pins; the tables of matching mohair shirts and sweaters, and shoulder bags bursting with notes and cosmetics, the girls who had only their failures in common, and the ones who sat together in victory feasting. Some tables, a few, were boy-girl, but mostly there was segregation—the boys set apart from the girls, and the popular from those who weren't. Oddly, we all knew our places, what seats we were destined to sit in. I remember once a lunch hour bake sale took away three tables, leaving a group of confused ninth graders with voices not yet changed and legs too long for their elastic-waisted corduroy trousers. They moved one table back to where the senior boys, the ones with flasks of Bourbon in their lunch bags, normally sat. Like a delicate marshland environment, our whole ecology, our structure collapsed that day.

How do kids decide, as they invariably do, which people to admire and which ones to ignore or laugh at? It's more than looks (good looks often happen *after* popularity, in the happy confidence that comes from admiration). Anyway, beauty, real beauty, wasn't all that successful at my school, any more than grades over B+ were. Cuteness, on the other hand, was fine—for girls *and* boys—especially in junior high, when too much tough male handsomeness comes frighteningly close to big-league sex. It's been the making of all those junior high-style idols—Bobby Sherman, the Monkees, David Cassidy. I'd study girls' faces and imagine how they looked just out of bed, still puffy-eyed, before mascara. Besides the button noses and clean hair (a shampoo every night) there wasn't much that make-up couldn't manufacture.

If nobody at Oyster River especially longed to be anything as uncomfortably extreme as *beautiful*, everybody, but everybody, very much wanted to be Good-Looking, and preferably terrifically Good-Looking. Most of us thought it had a lot to do with clothes and make-up, but the instincts—to know *which* make-up, how to look as

if you really didn't care and it was just by accident that
peach blusher brushed across your cheeks, like a leaf or
a wind—that was the rare thing and the thing that,
unlike looks, you had to be born with. Some girls would
try too hard and end up with lipstick on their teeth, a
place around the jawline where, like a mask, the make-up
color ended and the skin began and notes circulating
about them—"What's she trying to look like, a fashion
model?"

For a boy to be Good-Looking, it was mainly a matter
of how to look as if you didn't care how you looked, and
still·look good. It was the ability to wear a tucked-in shirt
(the overblouse, shirttail effect always resembled the styles
worn by pregnant women) and still not come off short-
waisted and stilt-legged. A dozen accidents of pure luck
entered in—how a boy took his liquor (one sick messy
drunk, or three, might haunt him forever) and when the
choir-boy lilt changed to a grunting bass, and how much
squeaking and warbling came between the two. One boy I
remember stayed locked into that halfway period from
seventh grade through twelfth, never sure, ahead of time,
which way his voice would come out when he spoke.
Sometimes it yodeled from one octave to another, or
broke off altogether so he'd mouth the word and nothing
came. He ended up not saying anything, of course, for
which one unobservant teacher penalized him heavily and
finally put him back a grade, so that his station in the
school, like his sad, thin voice, remained in limbo for another year.

Sometimes the body alone killed one's chances to be
good-looking or attractive. There were boys with girlish
hips (and I'm afraid we walked behind and imitated them)
and there were girls whose legs and arms were boyish.
There were girls who, from third grade on, hunched over
with the weight and shame of early bras—I remember the
shadow that showed through under white blouses, and the
moment, each September in the locker room, when we
pulled off our shirts and revealed just what had happened
over the summer and just who would join the club. For
some that moment came too early and for others, like
me—scrambling frantically in the bathroom to get my
gym suit on, snapping the fasteners that concealed an un-

dershirt, while lines of girls formed outside the door and
called "Hurry up in there, I've gotta go"—it came fatally
late.

Before describing what seemed for years a hopeless career
at sports, a never-ending battle between myself and The
Ball (base-, foot-, or volley-)—before doing all that, my
pride and vanity demands an interjection into present
time. So, for whatever it's worth, or for all the other
struck-out, last-to-be-chosen, ball-fumbling, race-losing
gym class failures, I want to say that I know now I'm *not*
a total washout at sports; I *can* run and swim and throw a
ball; I can do sit-ups and jumping jacks (it always seemed
a marvel of co-ordination, getting your legs and arms to
work at the same time like that). But what athletic
prowess I have now comes not because of, but in spite of,
elementary and junior high and high school gym.

I don't think people who are athletic can understand
people who aren't, as people with a gift for music just
can't comprehend what tone deafness would be like. All
through those years, I feared and dreaded gym class and
expended more effort in trying to get out of it than would
have been required if I'd gone. I forged medical excuses
and said I'd lost my sneakers ("so borrow some," the
teacher said, and for the next hour I clumped around in
someone else's smelly shoes). I hid in closets, I said I was
getting adjusted to contact lenses, or nauseous or that I
had cramps—this every two weeks or so, until the teacher
caught on and started keeping records. It was my early
failures on the playground—tripping when I jump-roped
Pepper, freezing at the top of the slide, unable to go down
and having to retreat finally, down the ladder I'd mounted
so nervously, all those things made me decide, by age
eight, that I was what at our school was called *spastic*
("no offense," they'd say)—a flop at all things physical.
And once you decide you are, or let other people decide it
for you, you become so. Those who are labeled unco-ordinated grow worse every year from nerves and lack of
practice (no one picks them when teams are chosen up,
and once they've been dealt out, their team captain juggles
the batting order so they never have to play).

By sixth grade, when we started having gym class three

times a week and playing more than volleyball, I stopped questioning the fact that I was unco-ordinated and accepted my role as bench warmer and occasional team comedian, a guaranteed laugh whenever I went up to bat or tried to dribble down the basketball court. That rarely happened though—kids knew better than to toss the ball to me. Running back and forth, up and down the gym to chase a ball that I would never catch seemed pointless to me, so I took to giving myself little rests—sitting down on the goal line or drifting off into the woods when I played the outfield. My teammates must have been relieved to see me go, but the gym teachers never gave up, each one clearly hoping that she would be the one to break through to me, each one taking my failures as a personal insult to her.

Gym teachers were forever trying to bring out something that wasn't there. It wasn't just that my muscles seemed improperly strung and my stamina lacking, my problem lay in the fact that I simply didn't care. Oh, I cared a great deal about looking clumsy as I struggled up the climbing rope and ran, knees knocking, to first base on the pinch-hit home run made by a friend. I cared, when teams were chosen, that I was picked last or dealt out like a handicap to whichever seemed the better team. But I had no feeling for nets and baskets and spinning, bouncing leather-covered spheres. I never felt, when watching a game, the way suspenseful books and movies make me feel—tense and excited, muttering under my breath (a cinematic cheerleader) "Come on, you can do it. Hurry up!"

One thing that saved me was that the class "nummers," "retards," "spastics" like me always came in pairs. All through the years I spent at war with balls and gym teachers, I had an ally. Sometimes she would be the class fat girl or someone born with a leg that never grew right, or a poor girl from the country with wishbone legs and bangs that fell down in her eyes and no real gym suit, which was (I suspected) the real reason why she didn't play. Most often my companion on the outfield would be a borderline outsider like me, someone who wrote poetry or got talked about for her funny hand-me-downs, or a hysterical giggler who chewed her nails and wrote dirty jokes with me in study hall.

The way athletic competence had been distributed among us always fascinated me. It happened too often to be a coincidence, that the same people who were cool and cute-looking and bright (in an unthreatening way)—and popular—were the ones who got picked first, were, in fact, the captains of the teams. Their grace—no, it was ease, really, and confidence—seemed to be transferable from one part of life to another. The line between Winners and Losers cut through all phases of school life almost from kindergarten on, and to cross it was as hard as kicking the ball past the goal posts. At age thirteen I felt my life was fated from then on—I saw the pattern that had followed me so far as never-changing right up to my death. That was what frightened and discouraged me most about phys. ed.—the feeling (reinforced at every step) that I was a loser. It seemed as though the sole object of those classes was to chip away the ego, bit by bit. I felt it on the baseball field and at the spider ball net, stumbling through the obstacle course (alone, the whole class watching) and back in the locker room, where even my sweatlessness pointed to my inadequacy, where the jaunty, casual talk in the great open shower stall (it comes to me in nightmares still—a gas chamber) made me blush, where the weekly inspection to make sure we'd really showered sent me fleeing to the bathroom stalls (I'd bared myself enough in class without adding the shame of a flat chest to my list of failures), where even opening the combination lock of a locker was impossible for me.

The very way you walked was important, not to the ones who did it right—they never had to think about it or to practice, their shoes were never worn more on one side than on the other—but to the ones who didn't, the ones who bounced or swayed or slumped. I was aware of almost every step I took, imagined mirrors and heavy clumping sounds. I envied ballerinas, and studied the girls at school whose walking I admired to see just how they swung their arms and where they put their chins and shoulders. That was something I did a lot—checking to see how the others, the very popular ones, did things—

how they chewed their lunch-box carrot sticks, whether they wore loafers with pennies in them or not (not—penny loafers were corny), and whether, on rainy days, they put on rubbers or got their feet soaked. But like that storybook character who brings his mother milk when she asks for eggs, eggs when she asks for flour, flour when she wants milk, no matter what I learned from my study of The Popular, I seemed to be forever one step out of time.

Never positively unpopular, I hung around the fringes, moving in just occasionally to become a student council secretary or dance decorations chairman. The logical train of thought that put me in office was the same kind by which people assume that if a man paints still lifes and landscapes well, surely he can do walls and fences; if I could write poetry—awful stuff, too—surely I'd be perfect for writing minutes.

I used to blame it on my name, the hissing at the end of my one syllable, the impossibility of abbreviating what was, itself, a kind of abbreviation, and the awkwardness of adding y or ie or, as some girls did, when they hit junior high, the letter i. If I had been Debbie or Cyndi or Kathy or Sally—Deb or Cind or Kath or Sal ... well, things would have been different. Sometimes, usually in September, when a new teacher and a new bunch of kids gave me—briefly—the illusion of a fresh start, I'd try a nickname, instructing my parents and my best friend, Becky, to call me (oh God!) Cricket or Pumpkin or D.J. On the first day of school, as the roll call was read, it seemed to me that there was plenty in a name, all right. The LuAnns and Franceses of the fourth grade would sink, one always knew, and from the moment when red-haired Margie Taylor's name was read (it happened every year: "Mary Margaret" the teacher would say ... mock horror from the class, then giggles, "Margie, she means *you*," and a long, funny cute-dumb explanation, "Well, my parents named me Mary, but . . ."), from that moment, we knew that Margie had it made.

By fifth or sixth grade I had learned that new haircuts and bobby-pin curls and red underpants would make no difference, and I became—in the name department, any-way—almost humble, flattered when a boy or a big kid (seventh grade) called me by name, because it meant

that he acknowledged my existence, he recognized and
accepted a decision made by my parents twelve years before. Even boys' not bumping into me as we passed in the
halls came to seem a compliment. They saw me, they had
not ignored me, and they—those celebrities whose discarded lunch bags, even, seemed special to me—they had
altered their course down the hallway to allow for *me*.

It was reverse logic, really, my plan to change my
name, my walk, my parents—to copy the kids who
seemed always right, the popular ones. I longed for the
kind of parents who played bridge and went to PTA and
took me camping and bowling. Or, more precisely, I
longed not to have a different set of parents who did those
things but—contradiction in terms—I wished my own parents would do them. They went along with me—they tried
bowling, even (and it is one of my favorite images of
them: my father in his tie and jacket, reluctant to let go
of the ball, rolling it slowly so as not to chip the pins; my
mother lobbing it energetically into one gutter or the other
and making an occasional strike), but of course they put
the label of our strangeness on their bowling so that, far
from making us more *normal*—like those families on
TV—it only pointed up how different we were. I came to
see, finally, that the parents of the Kathys and Cindys and
Debbies of the world were what I called *right* (by that I
meant they fitted in, everything they did seemed properly
American) not because they did things like bowling, but
that they did things like bowling because they were, from
the core, *right*. Whatever they had done, because they did
it, would have seemed fitting. When I affected their actions I was imitating effects instead of causes, so of course
I failed.

1965

Ask us whose face is on the five-dollar bill and we may not know the answer. But nearly everyone my age remembers a cover of *Life* magazine that came out in the fall of 1965, part of a series of photographs that enter my dreams and my nightmares still. They were the first shots ever taken of an unborn fetus, curled up tightly in a sack of veins and membranes, with blue fingernails and almost transparent skin that made the pictures look like double exposures. More than the moon photographs a few years later, that grotesque figure fascinated me as the map of a new territory. It was often that way with photographs in *Life*—the issue that reported on the *In Cold Blood* murders; a single picture of a boy falling from an airplane and another of a woman who had lost two hundred pounds. (I remember the faces of victims and killers from eight years ago, while the endless issues on Rome and nature studies are entirely lost.)

Photographs are the illustrations for a decade of experiences. Just as, when we think of *Alice in Wonderland* we all see Tenniel's drawings, and when we think of the Cowardly Lion we all see Bert Lahr, so, when we think of

Lyndon Johnson's air-borne swearing-in as president in 1963, we have a common image furnished by magazines. And when we think of fetuses, now, those cabbages and smiling, golden-haired cherubs have been replaced forever by the cover of *Life*. Having had so many pictures to grow up with, we share a common visual idiom and have far less room for personal vision. The movie versions of books decide for us what our heroes and villains will look like, and we are powerless to change the camera's decree. So, while I was stunned and fascinated by that eerie fetus (where is he now, I wonder, and are those pictures in his family album?) I'm saddened, too, knowing what it did to me. If I were asked to pinpoint major moments in my growing up, experiences that changed me, the sight of that photograph would be one.

I AM a magazine and paperback reader, but most of all a television watcher. What I think of as a uniquely American brand of banality fascinates me. In bookstores I pick up paperbacks and check before I buy to see if the characters have foreign names, whether the action takes place in London or New York. Intellectual friends (who watch no TV) can't understand what I see in reruns of old Andy Griffith shows. "Nothing happens," they say. "The characters are dull, plastic, faceless. Every show is the same." I guess that's why I watch them—boring repetition is, itself, a rhythm—a steady pulse of flashing Coca-Cola signs, Holiday Inn signs, and the Golden Arches of McDonald's.

I don't watch TV as an anthropologist, rising loftily above my subject to analyze. Neither do I watch, as some kids now tune in to reruns of "The Lone Ranger" and "Superman" (in the same spirit they enjoy comic books and pop art) for their camp. I watch in earnest. How can I do anything else? Five thousand hours of my life have gone into this box.

I was an undiscriminating television viewer who would

sometimes sit down before the set at three o'clock, when I
got home from school, and not get up again till dinner,
not even to change the channels. I let it all pour over
me—the quiz shows and the soap operas, old movies and
Westerns, but what I liked best were the situation comedies. I followed them all—"The Beverly Hillbillies," "My
Favorite Martian," "The Flying Nun," "My Mother the
Car"—with a certain assurance at the start of each show
that exaggeration, broad or narrow, dry or wet, was to
follow, that bathtubs would not just overflow, they would
fill the house with soap bubbles; that ghosts would levitate
objects for the benefit of someone's boss, who had so little
confidence in his own sanity that this would be enough to
drive him near the brink—his nervous breakdowns were
supposed to make us smile; that a nun could fly, a witch
would marry a mortal, a horse would talk and some out-
landish figure would move into someone's otherwise-nor-
mal suburban home—a martian, a genie, a woman reincarnated as a 1933 Ford. The very farfetched shows—the
ones whose plots hinged on some outside improbability—I
watched, but never completely enjoyed, just as I never
liked the way comic books and cartoons made me feel,
and never cared for the broad, punch-me humor of "The
Three Stooges." Their exaggeration seemed like mockery,
too stylized, too far removed from any recognizable human motive.

What I liked best of all were the quiet, often dull family
situations whose fascination for me lay in their comfortable unremarkableness. A few contained genuine comic
spark of course ("I Love Lucy," the old "Dick Van Dyke
Show," "The Andy Griffith Show"), and those I watched
for the performances, conscious of being entertained, and
of Lucille Ball's silly-putty mouth and Dick Van Dyke's
graceful awkwardness, as he tripped, weekly, over the
steps in his split-level and into the arms of Mary Tyler
Moore. The other shows, though—the forgotten half-hours
that died in midseason, and the ones, like "The Real
McCoys," "Father Knows Best," "Ozzie and Harriet,"
"Make Room for Daddy," that went on, like breathing,
forever, so that the children grew up before our eyes,
while the fathers balded and the mothers went gray—
those gave me another sort of satisfaction. They made the

eventlessness of my own life, the eventlessness that had brought me to the set in the first place, seem comfortingly acceptable.

Anyone can see comedy—or Komedy—in the levitations of a martian or the exaggerated dress and accent of a millionaire hillbilly. What a show like "Leave It To Beaver" did was harder—it made everydayness entertaining, even beguiling, it seemed to put a comic frame around my kind of life, tended to magnify the everyday situation (or to present it, unmagnified, in all its dilution, as if the camera had simply recorded any random half-hour at the Cleaver house). I loved "Leave It To Beaver"; I saw every episode two or three times, witnessed Beaver's aging, his legs getting longer and his voice lower, only to start all over again with young Beaver every fall. (Someone told me recently that the boy who played Beaver Cleaver died in Vietnam. The news was a shock, the first thing that had made the war seem real to me. I kept coming back to it for days, until another distressed Beaver fan told me that it wasn't true after all.)

We watched Westerns and police dramas for vicarious excitement, to see, from our armchairs, as observers, scenes we would never in life be part of, and so there was a necessary sadness to the act of watching, coming from the knowledge that people like the ones the show portrayed would never need to watch TV. But there was nothing vicarious about watching Bud Anderson or Ricky Nelson or Patty Duke—even the names are forgettable, beside "The Man from U.N.C.L.E.'s" Napoleon Solo, or Zorro. The Bud Andersons of the world watched TV too, it was clear, so seeing them on TV was rather like seeing ourselves. Not that the situation comedies were realistic—our kitchen at home never looked like Donna Reed's—but they were at least fascinatingly ordinary. Too much realism would have jarred; things in real life never have that reassuring television symmetry, soothing as the ticking of a clock.

I remember the one time, in all my years of viewing, when a TV family seemed to break the code of what's supposed to happen on TV and what isn't. The actress playing Danny Thomas's wife on "Make Room for Daddy" must actually have died, or just got tired of playing Mom to Sherry and Rusty. At any rate, whatever really happened, on one truly shaking episode, her absence was explained to the children by a wet-eyed Daddy, who said that Mom had gone to Heaven. I knew it was just a TV show, of course, but *that* kind of thing wasn't supposed to happen on *this* kind of TV. A rule had been broken, or alarmingly bent, and it seemed as if, after that, I could have faith in little else I saw.

When I was eight or nine, I first heard the phrase "Stop the World, I Want to Get Off." I remember perfectly the moment when I read the words for the first time, in an advertisement, and stopped dead in my skimming of the Sunday *Times*. It was, I think, one of my first real encounters with what I called then "deep thinking" (the other times came when I first considered Death—my own, negative numbers and "What came first, the chicken or the egg?"). That Stop-the-World phrase, anyway, seemed so familiar, and so telling, struck so deep, it was as if I'd thought it up myself. I knew the feeling, all right—the frightening, exhausting realization that no matter what, from now till my death, *I could not really take a rest*. It isn't the exclusive possession of kids in my generation, I'm sure—this treadmill feeling—but we grew up, certainly, during a time when the feeling was especially strong, a time that was, in an awesome variety of ways, hectic. We were worn out a bit by all the fireworks around us—space shots and wars and new music and new dances and new drugs. They were too exciting not to watch, and yet we hoped for an unexciting intermission that never seemed to come. TV programs, like the bland half-hour shows I loved, gave us that rest—more so, even, than books or sleep; in books you're left to visualize characters, while the all-inclusive camera leaves no room for the imagination or the editing of detail. (Not even our dreams are free from activity and pressure. Even as we dream them, we evaluate and censor.)

It may sound lofty and rationalizing to say this, but I think I watched and watch still, rapt, those situation comedies for the same reason that some of the more mystically minded of my generation have turned to meditation. (The meditator's goal always seemed an odd one to me: the ultimate experience reportedly being to stare at a glass of water and think nothing, nothing whatever; not "glass" or "water" or "What will I have for dinner tonight?"—to empty the mind, or at the very least to make a blank of it.) That seems to me just what I did watching TV, I realize now; in Zen terms (the Zen masters would be horrified, I guess) I ceased meditation. There was nothing that needed to be thought about during the blandest shows. (Bland, but not charmless. When charm left, the show made its presence felt again, like yeastless dough, heavy in the stomach. "How did that girl get her part?" I'd wonder. "Who wrote that terrible script?" And the lovely, mindless coasting feeling would be gone.) When the Douglasses or the Nelsons or the Petries or the Ricardos or the Stones were in true form, though, I didn't ever wonder how the show would turn out, or why anyone was doing what he did. Like pleasant grade-B detective stories I read with no desire to turn first to the last page and find out what happens, I never felt suspense as to how "The Donna Reed Show" would turn out. If I'd seen a show before, it didn't matter, because every show was a replay of the classic pattern anyway, and I could see them over and over just as I can hear the refrain to a song time and again.

Not just the outcomes, either, but the whole world the characters inhabited was reassuringly familiar. I knew where Harriet Nelson kept her stainless steel and where the phone was at the Petries' house and where Beaver Cleaver sat at the dinner table before he left it (his pie untouched), as he always did when he was in trouble, with "Uh, Mom, could I be 'scused?" I got so I could predict punch lines and endings, not really knowing whether I'd seen the episode before or only watched one like it. There was the bowling ball routine, for instance: Lucy, Dobie Gillis, Pete and Gladys, they all used it. Somebody would get his finger stuck in a bowling ball (Lucy later updated the gimmick using Liz Taylor's ring) and then they'd have to go to a wedding or give a speech at the PTA or have the boss to dinner, concealing one hand all the while.

We weren't supposed to ask questions like "Why don't they just tell the truth?" These shows were built on deviousness, on the longest distance between two points, and on a kind of symmetry which decrees that no loose ends shall be left untied, no lingering doubts allowed. (The surgeon general is off the track in worrying about TV violence, I think. I grew up in the days before lawmen became peacemakers. What carries over, though, is not the gunfights but the optimism that shone through all those hours spent in the shadows of the TV room, the memory that everything always turned out all right.)

Motivations stemmed from the most basic things in human nature and so I recognized all that I saw from what I knew of myself. The way Beaver tried to look jaunty, tossing his cap in the air and swinging his lunch box, hoping to conceal the weight of the bad report card inside, the way Dick Van Dyke crossed and uncrossed his legs when he was nervous and rubbed his chin and scrunched his hands deep in his pockets so that his shoulders came up, the way Patty Duke arranged her face just to talk on the telephone, and the way her dumb-nice boy friend Richard looked when he ate a cake she'd made for him and burned —showing us that it tasted awful at the same time he was trying to show her how much he liked it, which showed us how much he must like her.

There was a congruence to everything that happened on those shows, so that the outcome seemed fated, which excused my passivity and powerlessness as I lay stretched out on the sofa for hours on end, eating grapes, experimenting with red nail polish. (Thy will be done, and not a thing I could do about it, even if I tried—reason enough not to bother.) It was all unstoppable. Steve Douglass would have three sons, one of whom would marry and become the father of, naturally, triplets—three sons. Desi would give Lucy a new dress for Christmas, and he'd be sure to find that Fred Mertz next door had bought one just like it for Ethel. Everything fell into place, just about geometrically, yet watching it happen never seemed dull.

Many people are shocked and dismayed by the tranquilizing sameness of so many TV shows, I know. They call TV "the boob tube" and speak of the apathy and passivity they feel it produces in young all-day viewers, and often they're right, it does. I think a lot depends on how a parent guides his children through the television experience, and the dangers brought on by too much easy-chair safety. If all that TV comedies did was to provide us with was a

E VERYBODY has one somewhere in his memory of growing up—a death remembered, a date whose anniversary you note each year (one year ago today . . . two . . .), a place on some highway whose skid marks remind you, a yearbook page, edged in black, "in memory of"—even listing them sounds sentimental and tear-jerking; as the word "prom" carries instant connotations, so does the mention of crashed cars and memorial scholarships. We go back to them at odd times—late at night and full of beer, on New Year's Eve, in thunderstorms—and tell the story over and over again; like "the night I lost my virginity," it comes up: your first encounter with death. Grandparents and distant relatives are rarely mentioned—they may be loved, but old people are supposed to die; there's sadness, but no real shock in that. It's the death of another young person—maybe one you barely knew—that comes back.

I don't think I was abnormally death-possessed, but I thought about it a lot. I worried about my own death, of course, and was fascinated by the deaths of others—people my own age especially. I turned to the newspaper obituary column first thing every day, before Ann Landers and the comics, even, to see if someone young had died, and when they had, I read the announcement several times for any scrap that would reveal what death was like. I pieced together everything I could, hoping to find a clue. "In lieu of flowers, donations may be sent to the Cancer Society . . ." was self-explanatory; "after a long illness . . ." meant homework missed, a teacher's visits, maybe, with workbook pages to fill out, or letters sent from everyone at school, composed by the teacher, written on the board and copied by the class, graded for penmanship and sent with a paint-by-number kit they'd all chipped in to buy; "the infant son of" filled my mind, and our recess-time discussions, with visions of failed incubators and quarter-sized coffins. I mulled the details, studied the faces of the mourners, with what must seem cruel fascination. All children do it though. (I had a friend whose parents had forbidden her to say "death" or any word related to it around her younger brother, which didn't stop his knowing about it, of course, or his thinking about it, but only kept the fear nameless.) It seems a necessary process, the only way to learn about death—getting shocked and shaken until you reach the point where it no longer takes you by surprise, when death seems, finally, natural. It took me years of obituary-reading to arrive at that point, if I am there yet.

Slowly, at least, I reached the realization that I could go at any moment and that, though I was not allowed to stay up past eight-thirty or ride my bike on the highway, though I didn't own more than half a dozen Kennedy half-dollars and a few dolls and books, I *did* own something as awesome as my life, and had the power to end it. I had only to stick my wet hand in the light bulb socket, to close the garage door while the car warmed up on winter mornings or, a little later, when I could drive, to swerve the steering wheel just half a turn, into the left hand lane, and I could bring about a change more catastrophic, to my family, at least, than anything the President or the Russians could accomplish. It wasn't that I ever considered suicide (though most of us have contemplated it in childhood—after a spanking or a banishment, the momentary thought of "Boy, could I show them . . . !");

what fascinated me about death was that I could bring it about *myself*.

I talked about it, thought about it, studied all evidences of it that I could find, hoping, I guess, that by constant exposure I'd get accustomed to the idea. Walking home from school, after a little boy who lived nearby us had been run over and killed, Becky and I would ponder God and The Universe. (Death always led to discussions of the solar system. Fourth-grade science merged with theology, so that I pictured heaven—not that I really believed, but just in case—somewhere above the rings of Saturn, orbited by a moon, while hell lay ninety-three million miles away in the corona of the sun.) And then, abruptly, we'd switch to the earthly details of the death—"What do you think the little boy's teacher will do about his name written up on the reading group chart? Will she cross it out or leave it there? What are his parents doing now? Will they eat supper? Do you think they'll give away his toys? Would *you* want them?" The possessions of a dead person, the beds they slept in, the chairs they'd sat on, seemed to carry the contagion of death. We knew there were no germs, no viruses attached to car accidents and cancers, but we avoided certain spots of road and certain cafeteria seats anyway, full of the supersitions we all carry about death, bred from its strangeness.

There couldn't have been many twelve-year-olds in 1966 or so who ever missed watching "Dr. Kildare." Not because of Kildare himself—Richard Chamberlain seemed a white-coated neutral quantity to us—but because of the far greater appeal of death and disease. Oh, we bore with him when he took a week every so often to fall in love (once it lasted four consecutive episodes—an Italian romance—and we grew impatient) but what we really loved were the cancer weeks, the amputations, the blindnesses. True, the unhappy patients were only actors giving their all to a juicy part, but I studied their faces anyway to catch a glimpse of death. Those episodes I remember perfectly; they were discussed beforehand from what scraps the previews gave us, prepared for with a fresh batch of chocolate chips or brownies, and watched together sometimes with a next-door-neighbor friend, so we could hug ourselves that it wasn't us who had only three months to live. I remember the beautiful surfer girl who discovered she had epilepsy, was forbidden to surf and disobeyed Kildare (we saw him in bathing trunks that week) to take her final wave, eyeballs rolling, and die.

There was the full-grown man who'd lost the power of speech and was reduced to baby talk until, after a night-long session with Kildare, sitting before a mirror mouthing syllables, he came out with the barely comprehensible sound of his wife's name. (The idea of an adult mind imprisoned in an infantile clumsiness of speech fascinated all of us. When I reminisce with friends about old Kildare shows, they often mention that one. I think it touched on real and thrilling childhood fantasies—the man-baby, to-tally stripped of dignity as children are so often stripped of theirs.) That ending was presented as a happy one (much to my disappointment, they usually were; patients rarely died) but what we liked about it was the fundamental bleakness of the resolution.

Another time a teen-age girl lost one eye in a car accident (with her no-good boy friend at the wheel). She didn't know, at first, that the eye had been taken out, under all those bandages (shades of my all-time favorite childhood movie moment, when Ronald Reagan wakes up, cheerful after an operation by a quack doctor, looks under the sheet and says, "Hey, you cut off my leg!"). Then, after she realized what happened, there were fittings for a glass eye, instructions in using it, then a reuniting with the boy, who loved her even more this way. (Once again, though I knew the actress hadn't really lost an eye, I watched her face to see if I could tell the difference.) It was all part of accustoming myself to accident and death, searching for the scraps of clues the Kildare shows gave us to what death was really like.

It must seem that we were morbid, and we were. My friends and I pored over Life magazine whenever it ran photographs of war amputees or thalidomide babies or Siamese twins. Terrible accidents held the same power for us—I remember the photographs Life ran of the Flying Wallendas, moments before their fall, and one eery shot of an airplane stowaway, a teen-age boy, falling from the plane as it took off, and frozen in mid-air, far enough from the ground, I told myself and shivered, to have had time to think. Oh, and the murders. Richard Speck and the eight nurses, the *In Cold Blood* slaughter and, years later, (I, ashamed now of my interest), the Charles Manson-Sharon Tate killings, the worst of all. The victims' old yearbook photographs and their ironic near-escapes ("She decided, at the last minute, to stay home . . .") all tantalized us. ("What if . . ." and "if only . ." we murmured.)

The truth was that, though we never would have admitted it, we thrived like vampire bats on these catastrophes—expected them. They gave our lives suspense—who will be next?—and made us thrill at our miraculous survival, imagining dangers and close calls. ("Just think," a friend told me, "I was in Chicago just two months before those nurse murders. It could've been me.") We all felt newly desirable, the possessors of something—life, and virginity—that every rapist/murderer wants. Violence and danger lurked in every corner, cancer in every glass of diet cola, blindness in every sporty red convertible. So—by the obscure workings of twelve-year-old logic—we all felt safer, snug in our beds the way a flannel-pajama-ed, quilted sleeper feels when he can hear the storm winds rage outside.

I CAN'T say that none of us read books, but certainly we weren't a Generation of Readers. We never *had* to read—there was always TV, and so we grew accustomed to having our pictures presented to us, our characters described on the screen more satisfactorily, it seemed to many of us, than five pages of adjectives. Once accustomed to television, we were impatient with book dramas: they moved so slowly, took so much effort, required us to visualize things and cluttered the story, as I saw it then, with the superfluous details writers put in only to please English teachers. I skipped over descriptions of people's eyes or their sitting rooms or the sunsets they walked through, moving instead straight to the action, which could never compete with what I got watching "Highway Patrol" and "Wagon Train." Having witnessed on the screen whole armies marching, lions moving in on their prey, ghosts, monsters, witches, Martians, nothing that we merely read about could shake us much. Anybody could *tell* us on paper that something happened (showing it on TV was more respected) but how could we believe it just from wordy hearsay? And for us, believing—having the conviction that what we read was really true—mattered a lot.

Because the main function of television and movies was, for us, to get the story told, we came to see the arrival, and not so much the journey, as the important part of all fictions—of everything in life, in fact. We are outcome-conscious, we watch or read to see how it all turns out, just as we play to win (it isn't *really*, we all know, how you play the game that matters) and enter college to graduate, and graduate to get a job or to get into graduate school. So the purpose of books seemed often simply to move us toward the ending, and if we could have read the last page without plowing through all the others and still have understood what happened, we would have done it.

When we read the book it was because we couldn't see the movie, or because we'd seen it already and wanted to recapture something of the movie experience. (Just as you read a keepsake menu, sometimes, to summon the memory of a good meal.) We'd open *Gone With the Wind* knowing what Scarlett O'Hara looked like, and what color her dresses were in every scene, and how Melanie wore her hair. The easy short-cut method of description made possible by cameras came to influence our writing and our speech, I think. We lost something of the power to describe from scratch because we no longer needed to. Instead of telling what a friend looks like, we have only to show his photograph and say "He's really great." Or that he looks exactly like Steve McQueen. One picture is worth a thousand words. Sometimes we read books less to evoke the characters and settings than to evoke the theater we saw the movie in.

I ordered stacks of school book club paperbacks, "for junior readers," each month—abridged classics, joke books, high school romances, biographies (Clara Barton—Angel of the Battlefield, Nellie Bly—Reporter. Wernher von Braun, I seem to remember, was Father of Rocketry, or maybe King of Lightning). I lined them up along my bookshelves (alphabetically, by author), but few were ever read. What I liked best was the *idea* of reading. Wrapped up in quilts before the fireplace, with thunder and lightning pounding outside, and a cup of cocoa or an apple or a bowl of popcorn in one hand, *Nancy Drew and the Hidden Staircase* in the other, I would stop and think, every other sentence, how nice this was, and that I should do it more often. Like a kid on a rusty Ferris wheel at a just-about-deserted amusement park, screaming "Isn't this fun?" more in an attempt to believe than in the conviction it was true. I got my pleasure from the image I'd acquired (on TV and in the movies) that things like this were full of *atmosphere.* The act itself—moving my eyes across the page—almost always put me to sleep. Even Nancy Drew seemed too abstract—words, no pictures.

From the dubious lessons of TV I'd swallowed the old saw that seeing was believing (and even in seeing, you had to take things with a grain of salt. Studying the TV superman as he flew and the announcer read, "It's a bird, it's a plane . . ." I had my doubts, searching for the piano wires I'd found in Mary Martin's *Peter Pan*, or evidence of trick photography. "He just lay down on a table, like he was flying," we decided). But as for books, less real-life, even, than film—why should I trust their honesty? And if they weren't honest and true to life, they were nothing. The improbability of Mr. Ed, the talking horse, was ten times greater than paperback biographies' distorted picture of Wernher von Braun, of course, but because the shows were acted out by real actors and a real horse, they seemed more immediate and therefore (by sixties-logic) more trustworthy.

Immediacy and newness were terribly important. That's what I liked about my book club paperbacks and why, if I didn't read them within the first week I got them, I never would; I liked new things—this year's copyright marks, just out this month, if possible. We were raised without much feeling for history and oldness, and books, to many of us, were like fashions. Anything written before 1960 seemed hopelessly out of date. We had little patience for last year's model (it isn't totally unrelated that every September found me battling for a new car—bucket seats, a sunroof, a "fastback"), and had no patience, as a rule, for anything predating us. As far as I was concerned, anyway, the world didn't exist until November 5, 1953, when I was born.

1966

When I think of 1966, I see pink and orange stripes and wild purple Paisleys and black and white vibrating to make the head ache. We were too young for drugs (they hadn't reached the junior high yet) but we didn't need them. Our world was psychedelic, our clothes and our make-up and our jewelry and our hairstyles were trips in themselves. It was the year of the gimmick, and what mattered was being noticed, which meant being wild and bright and having the shortest skirt and the whitest Yardley Slicker lips and the dangliest earrings. (We all pierced our ears that year. You can tell the girls who became teen-agers in 1966—they're the ones with not-quite healed over holes in their ears.) *Seventeen* that year was full of vinyl skirts, paper dresses, op and pop, Sassoon haircuts, Patty Duke flips and body painting. My own outfits would have glowed in the dark. I remember one, a poorboy top and mod Carnaby Street hat, a silver micro skirt and purple stockings. (Pantyhose hadn't been invented yet; among our other distinctions, call us the last generation to wear garter belts. I recall an agonizing seventh-period math class in which, ten minutes before the bell

rang, my front and back garters came simultaneously un-
done.)

It was as if we'd just discovered color, and all the shiny,
sterile things machines made possible for us. Now we cultivate the natural, homemade look, with earthy colors and
frayed, lumpy macramé sashes that no one would mistake
for store-bought. But back then we tried to look like
spacemen, distorting natural forms. Nature wasn't a van-
ishing treasure to us yet—it was a barrier to be overcome.
The highest compliment, the ultimate adjective, was *unreal*.

I NEVER remembered, in May, as I counted the days till school got out, what summer vacation was really like. After the excitement of the first swim and walking barefoot and going for picnics on our bikes, it came to us (each year, as if we'd hit on some new discovery) that school, much as we hated it, gave form to our lives. What summertime was meant for, more than anything else, was growing up. Soaking up sun and eating carrots so you'd have long hair—lightened, if you dared, with a lemon— when school began again. Summertime was when the changes happened, and why the first day of school was so much fun, with everybody telling everybody else how different they looked—and it was true.

Waiting for the changes to happen, though, was like watching corn grow. By August I would miss the tug of my leash and collar, with nothing, no commitments, to keep me from sleeping through the best hours of sunlight, rising late and eating soggy Cheerios by the TV set, glued there for hours (just one more program, I kept telling myself, still in pajamas) like an addict. After TV there might be waiting for the mail, then reading *TV Guide*—next week's menus—and all the advertising circulars the discount stores sent out. (Sales on men's underwear and clock radios I studied, rapt. I knew the retail price of everything, just as I came to know the stars of every TV show, the time it came on and the channel. My stores of useless summer information accumulated like algae in a swamp.) Often I'd look forward to rain—thunder storms especially—because it gave me an excuse to stay inside and make popcorn. Sometimes, when the sun was shining, I'd pull the blinds and feel guilty, or I'd rally to the weather, put on my bathing suit and bike to the town swimming pool, transplanted, in the space of half an hour, from stretched-out-on-the-couch to stretched-out-on-the-sand. Transistor radios were more in fashion then than now. (Now it is quiet we treasure. Back then it was little palm-sized boxes with wrist straps and earphones, held to the ears of teen-agers while they walked, as if without the sound of J. J. Jeffrey and his Solid Gold or Big Bud Ballou with this week's Top Ten, breathing would be impossible.)

Teen-agers seemed more *teen-age* then. They all seemed older-looking and more on top of things. It isn't true that the closer you get, the better things look. (I often think in TV jingle terms. My sentence rhythms come from Maybelline and Crest.) The closer I got to teen-age, the less grown up it seemed. Partly it was that college students came into their own during my teens (after years of isolationist scholarship, a sudden burst of *relevance*) so the action switched from us to them. It seemed unfair that I should have spent so long marking time, holding my place in line, sleeping (wake me up when I've grown up—that was my summer attitude) only to discover when finally I reached the ticket booth that no more seats were left or that, in fact, the concert had been canceled. A perpetual summer pre-teen, always on the brink, it seemed, I spent Junes, Julys and Augusts waiting for my bathing suit to fill out, for the time when I'd lie on a "Surf's Up" towel, or one that read "Drive Slow—No Parking—Soft Shoulders Ahead," rubbing suntan lotion into some lifeguard's back while, more romantic than violins, his transistor pounded out the Beach Boys' "Surfer Girl." Annette and Fabian, transistor radios and polka-dot bikinis, were gone by my first real teen-age summer. By then I dreamed of being college age and spent my summer as a babysitter, changing diapers.

For a time, a longish time, it seemed to be a pattern in my life that the boys who liked me were not the ones I cared about. It was never the student council members and the sports stars who asked me to dance (the kinds of boys I wanted, more than to be with, to be seen with, boys whose acceptance of me would, I felt, make me acceptable). Instead, I had the impression, and a fairly elaborate one, that I was attracting a whole series of school misfits like me, boys whose own out-ness reminded me of mine. If they danced awkwardly—and they did—it was not the stiff, cool awkwardness of a basketball player who can't afford to look too ballet-graceful, but the awkwardness of the boys who strike out in baseball and finish last, panting, in races. Looking back, it seems to me that my partners invariably danced with their mouths open. I can still see them loping across the dance floor to get me, presumably eager to lay sweaty palms on my organdy and velvet, bought for other, dryer hands.

I hated them, these misfits, for how alike we were. Seeing them, I imagined how I must have looked. I criticized them most of all for their taste in girls. For anyone I liked to like me back would make me like him less. Their having chosen me only went to show what losers they were.

It wasn't that I didn't have a pretty exalted opinion of myself—I did. The fact that I wasn't wildly popular puzzled me for a long time. I decided that we weren't seeing the same person—me, when I looked in the mirror, and the boys who said "Hey, did you get the license number of the tractor that ran over your face?" They convinced me finally that it must be so; if I wasn't ugly, I was at least different, odd-looking, and that was maybe even worse. Mine was not the kind of face that reminds people of faces on TV. And it was those smoothly smiling faces that were my models. My face impressed me not at all favorably, as untypical; I fell far short, I thought, of prettiness, and no amount of experimenting with clothes or hair styles or eyeshadow colors (each one just the barest

fraction of a shade different from the last) could turn
me into Gidget.

I grew up—we all did—to value the consensus. (What
sex is the baby rabbit? Let's take a vote . . .) My eye is
trained not to aesthetic absolutes but to the culturally accepted thing. (Are shaven legs and plucked eyebrows really more beautiful, or is it just the habit of seeing them
that way which makes me think they are?) My taste is no
longer my own—that much I know. I'm not a rider of
bandwagons, quite, but, much as I try to disregard them,
to think for myself, the opinions of other people matter to
me. I liked the kind of faces I saw in magazines, the kind
of boys who were well-liked by all, and while I didn't tor-
ment the ones many people made fun of, secretly I
thought less of them for having failed to win majority ap-
proval. I thought less of myself too, for my own lack of
popularity with boys, and so I scorned the boys who failed
to scorn me because they liked a face I didn't like, myself.

Why do looks *matter* so much?

I do not know a single girl who's really satisfied with
how she looks. Some toss their hair and smooth their
skirts and stride like models, and I'll start out envying
them and mentally exchanging faces or shapes or hair
color, but then I'll watch them looking at other girls as
they stride by tossing *their* hair, and I'll see, in the faces I
admired, the same sizing-up look that's on mine (how
much does she weigh? Does she color her hair? Curl her
eyelashes?) and realize that not one of us feels really *safe*.
I study my reflection in every full-length mirror and window and shiny toaster I pass (less from sheer vanity, I
think, than from insecurity, a dissatisfaction about the way
I look) and when I do examine myself, I almost always
see, reflected next to me, another insecure, dissatisfied girl
doing the same thing. We put on our mirror expressions
and glance hurriedly—sidelong, out of guilt—jumping a
little when discovered, bent over the sink in a department
store ladies' room, miming before the mirror. What we do
before mirrors is an intensely private act. We are examining and repairing the illusions we're attempting to
maintain (that *we* don't care about our looks, that how
we look when we look good is just a lucky accident) and

to be caught in mid-repair destroys the illusion. Like bald
men discovered with their toupees off, women viewed
early in the morning or at work before a mirror feel they
can never regain, in the eyes of those who see them—*before*—the image of how they look *after.*

Why do we feel like unwelcome strangers in our own
skins? I change clothes half a dozen times a day when I
feel at my worst, leaving pools of discarded costumes on
the floor, arranging myself in Outfit Number Nine, until,
at last, I'm reasonably pleased with how I look and then,
catching my image in a window two hours later, I find my
shakily assembled image has disappeared—I must change
again. I long for a face that I can count on; I'd like to
have eyes that are never puffy, a skin that's uniformly ol-
ive (not sallow, never sallow), hair that bounces and
emerges from convertibles and bike rides looking artfully
tousled instead of just plain lousy. It isn't necessarily
beauty I covet, but dependable attractiveness, a face I can
catch off guard and be happy at the sight of.

When I talk about it, all this must sound like a case-
book neurosis, but I think it's too commonplace to be
labeled an abnormality. It's our culture that has put a
premium on good looks—all the clothes designers and
hairdressers and department store buyers and magazine
editors, all aware, at least subconsciously, that we—
women—will suddenly and at long last escape the tyranny
of fashions on the very day we wholeheartedly *like* the
way we look. While constantly creating more products to
help us reach that point, they have managed to keep it always slightly beyond us. Just getting to a state of fashionable attractiveness is hard enough because fashions change
so quickly. Staying there is impossible. A newer, better
model is always around the corner—built-in obsoles-
cence—so that, no sooner do we buy a pair of suede hotpants, satisfying one season's requirements, than another
more pressing need is created (a patchwork skirt, an Ar-
gyle vest . . .). Our insecurity is what the beauty industry
depends on and encourages—the constant, one-step-be-
hind limbo we live in where each purchase, each haircut,
each diet is undertaken in the hopes that it will bring us
to some stable point where we can look in the mirror and
smile. Sometimes, of course, we do. Never for very long.

Pretty soon someone even better-looking passes by on the street, or on the TV screen or in a magazine, and the quest is on again.

Early on, magazines brought out the worst in me—greed and jealousy, wild competition. In *Seventeen* the clothes and make-up and the hairstyles fascinated me, but what really held me to the page was the models. In *Vogue* and *Glamour* they are anonymous, so the envy is at least targetless, generalized. But *Seventeen* models were, like the characters in monthly serials, old friends and some-times enemies. We knew their names, their beauty prob-lems ("Lucy's skin is oily, so she scrubs nightly with as-tringent soap and steams her face for that extra zing . . ."), their dieting secrets, their special touches. (Colleen would be "an individualist" one month, with a flower painted on her cheek or a tiny gold bracelet around the ankle. Next month we'd all be sporting ankle chains and cheek flowers.) What we remembered from the ads they posed in was not the brand of clothes they wore but what the girls who wore them looked like. I'd notice when a model had gained weight or when her stock seemed to be going down, when she was no longer one of the girls the magazine was on a first-name basis with, and—secretly, of course—these failures pleased me. Perhaps that's what the magazines depend on—our bitchiness and envy and our less-than-entirely joyful reaction to New York-style model beauty. We buy the magazine, study the models, to study the competition. Then if we like the way they look and, most important, feel envy, maybe we'll buy their outfits too.

It's not true of just me, I think, but of nearly every six-ties-bred girl, that no matter how bright or scholarly or talented or generally contented with her life she may be, she'll have some hidden weakness when it comes to models and modeling. To be loved for nothing but our looks, to make a living simply out of *being*, to be graceful and sweatless, cool and fashionable and most of all, looked at by other girls and envied—that is the hidden dream. The world is full of teen-age girls who long to model—short, plump, acne-scarred *Seventeen* readers who balance books on their heads behind closed doors or vamp in front of three-way mirrors, mouth slightly open, stomach forward, slouching, Twiggy style, toes in, knees knocking. Whatever our official goals, whatever we write on college applications, whatever we tell our parents that we plan to be when we grow up, the dream of modeling remains.

I went once to an agency, naïvely answering a want ad in the paper ("Glamorous modeling career?"). I was sixteen then, and my relatives had always told me "you could be a model." As soon as I arrived at the agency I saw I'd made a mistake, of course—all glass and chrome, with glossy pictures on all sides and deep shag rugs and a beautiful secretary (if *she* hadn't even made it as a model . . .) with one of the English, Carnaby Street accents that were so fashionable then. I had my interview anyway—a humiliating examination that made me feel ashamed of my presumptuousness to think, for even a moment, that I could be a model. I sensed, worse than contempt, my bell-bottomed, blue-booted interviewer's amusement. The agency's gambit was clear then—I'd pay them for a charm course and a set of photographs and for the privilege of being managed by them. I'd gone from employee to employer, with dazzling suddenness—asked to pay for their services as aging women hire gigolos.

So I abandoned my short-lived modeling career. I feel resentment still, slipping through fashion magazines, although I buy them all and never miss an issue. Love-hate is what it amounts to, I guess, and a little self-flagellation. My comfort lies in the knowledge that fashion models, like fashions, go out of style. The crop I grew up with has almost turned over—*Vogue* models live forever, sometimes, but *Seventeen* cover girls go on to modeling nurse's uniforms and pantsuits in Sears catalogues. I know their faces and their wig collections well—Terry and Cheryl, from my earliest days, then Lucy and Colleen, Twiggy, of course, Mona and Cybill. I wait in mean, small-minded anticipation for their mid-twenties. I haven't really conquered my envy, I've only passed it on from one set of smooth faces to another. All of which is a pretty sad and unliberated commentary on female nature (or, more likely, on our conditioning).

I can't quite bring myself to throw out my back issues of *Seventeen* magazine—every copy, since 1965, so worn sometimes, especially the fat August issues, full of back-to-school fashions and back-to-school hopes that This Year Will Be Different; beauty make-overs, exercises, tips for shiny teeth (rub them with Vaseline). I should want to be rid of them; they are what enslaved me to the conventions of fashion, what made me miserable about how I looked. Their pages were always full of clothes I couldn't afford and helpful hints that never really worked. (Talcum powder on the eyelashes—to make them look thicker—was gilding for a lily, not a dandelion.) Cucumbers over the eyes, lemon in the hair, face exercises to be done watching TV—I tried them all, rushing to the mirror when the miracle operations had been performed, expecting changes and finding only cucumber seeds stuck to my cheek and sticky, lemon-smelling hair no lighter than before.

My nights, from fifth grade through the ninth, were spent not so much sleeping as waiting for my hair to curl. I slept on plastic rollers and metal clips, in pincurls that left my hair squared off like wire, in hair nets and hairsprays and setting gels and conditioning oils, propped up on three pillows because the curlers hurt so much, or with my head turban-wrapped in toilet paper. I went through half a roll a night. Every morning I'd wake up with dark circles left under my eyes from a troubled half-sleep spent dreaming strange, curler-induced nightmares. I'd run to the mirror, when I woke, to unveil myself, never prepared—not even after all the other failed mornings when my efforts yielded only limp strands (or—worse—tight, greasy ringlets that would not come out) for a new disaster. Then I'd rip off the curls I'd stuck, with Scotch tape, to my face, arranging my hair so the red splotches left on my cheeks from the tape wouldn't show, and tease my hair, when teasing was still done, so the back of my skull looked enormous. It amazes me now to think that all those ugly styles I wore looked good to me back then. Will what I'm wearing now seem just as strange ten years from now, I wonder?

I was a slave to fashion—chopping off my hair one year to look like Twiggy, sweltering under a Dynel wig the year wigs were being worn, disappearing altogether for a while beneath an eye-obstructing curtain of bangs. Even when straight hair became fashionable, when girls slept on tin cans and ironed out their curls and when, presumably, I should have felt free to be myself, I felt, instead, the need to change my hair some other way—to alter the color or the length, to bleach a racing stripe down one side or tint it some other shade of brown, no better, maybe, but *different*. I grew up a believer in variety above all else, in quantity over quality, in "change of pace" (I heard that in a Lipton tea commercial and it stayed with me). No matter what you looked like, the way to improve your looks, I believed, was to change them. All through the sixties I fought nature, wore my face like a mask, my clothes like armor and my hair that pinned, clipped, rolled, taped, teased, washed, set, sprayed mass, meant to hang straight forever—I wore it like a hat.

Oh, the money that went into make-up! We never bought the cheap Woolworth's stuff, my friends and I, because you don't skimp on Beauty, and the more expensive the make-up, the better it must be. Mostly we paid for the packaging: blusher (that was 1960s talk for the unthinkable—rouge) in a tiny thumb-sized compact with a little swivel-out brush attached with a chain; false eyelashes that we never really wore except in the bathroom, packed in pastel carrying cases; lip glosses arranged like paints in a water-color box; face power with silver sparkles; cheekbone contour brushes to give us the emaciated look. Lipsticks sometimes came in flowerpots and doll shapes (that's what they were—toys, finger paints you applied to skin instead of paper). Eyeshadow swung in colored globes and psychedelic buckets from the belts in our hip-hugger bell bottoms.

Make-up was joyously synthetic back then, before the natural look, before organic skin creams and lipsticks whose aim was to be invisible and ads for "down to earth" cosmetics filled with genuine Arizona mud. It was the era of fads, white lips and rainbow eyelids and, for one brief period, an idea that never caught on—body painting. Yardley sold (or didn't sell, but tried to) buckets of purple, pink, orange and green paint and rollers to apply it with—to legs (instead of stockings) and arms (instead of sleeves) and even faces. No one at my school wore it because along with the desire to be the first one, to get no-

ticed, we were all afraid of going too far, and we stood
for hours in front of the mirror, making sure that our
see-through blouses (with strategically placed pockets)
didn't show too much, agonizing over the exposure of a
garter or a slip. ("Your slip is showing"—that dread whisper—always seemed a bit silly to me, when one of the big
fashion fads of that year was dresses with matching
bloomer-pantalets whose ruffle trailed at least an inch below the hem.) Those were loud, unsubtle, get-attention
days, when wild and crazy and eye-catching meant fashionable.

Days that added up to the junk era. Every decade has
its celluloid dolls and baseball cards, of course, and there
are plenty of them still—overpriced, overpackaged make-
up and flimsy toys that always look better in the cata-
logue, and breakfast cereals that taste like strawberry and
marshmallow and chocolate. But we are more quality-
conscious now, I think, aware, at least, of what it is we
lack, and longing for a return to natural ingredients, solid
old-fashioned construction and practical function. In the
sixties it always seemed that we had money to burn; our
quarters, like everything else, were disposable—you spent
what you got, and never thought of waiting for dimes to
become dollars, or dollars to turn into bank accounts. I
shopped for the sake of shopping, always looking for new
things that I didn't need, with new needs constantly being
invented. What I bought one Saturday would be gone by
the next. Giant plastic earrings, glow-in-the-dark Yo-yos,
posters, paper dresses, paper flowers, papier-mâché
bracelets, polka-dotted knee socks, issues of *Mad* magazine.

It was a time for fads, the little interval before what we
loved most was permanence. First Hula Hoops (two,
three, four at once—little ones for arms and ankles and
necks); mine always dropped early like horseshoes clang-
ing as they landed in the dust around their target. Then
there was Silly Putty, Super Balls, hi-riser bikes and bike
motors, whose only function was to make a noise
(Varooom!) when you rode, plastic trolls with glassy eyes
and long ratty hair; Vac-u-form mold sets and a machine
that made toys you could eat, and something called Super
Stuff, a pink powder you added water to until it made a

jelly-like pink goop. For about two weeks everybody at school had it. One boy I knew brought his stuff to Sunday school and threw it in the waist-length blond hair of a girl in his class, the kind of gesture that's as close as sixth-grade boys can come, perhaps, to demonstrating love. That day her hair was finally proved to be natural gold and not a dye job, as I, and the other mousy brunettes had hoped and hinted to the world—we had ample time, in the hours that followed, picking the Super Stuff out of her curls, to study the roots. (They were whiter than ever against the screaming pink of the Stuff.) We gave up in the end, and the girl got a haircut. About a month later I found my old bag of Super Stuff, with a funny green mold that seemed to be crawling all along the bottom.

And all that junk—the flashy make-up and jewelry and fashions and the gadgets—all that has affected even our eating. We are the snack food generation, raised on potato chips and Orange Crush, Cocoa Puffs and Froot Loops, popsicles and a new type of peanut butter (why, among all the other things, does this especially shock me?) that comes with marshmallow fluff mixed in, right in the jar. Our hamburgers are so well-done they're black, our orange juice is dehydrated, our vitamins come in the form of colored pills shaped like the Flintstones. Everything seems to be dried up or carbonated, colored, fancily packaged and, naturally, sugared.

The effects of all that on our physical well-being is bad enough, but what concerns me even more has to do with what all that junk-consuming, junk-food eating has done to us mentally and—if this doesn't sound too lofty—spiritually.

There is a slackness to our will, a numb, unthinking indifference in our grandstand munching—the way we reach for crackers on a plate simply because they're on it, the way we forget what flavor of ice cream we're licking, the way we finish a meal and can't remember if we've had dessert or not. ... And the gum, always that gum in our mouths, because even after the food is gone and the stomach filled, we still possess the need to *chew*. When—except when we diet, in which case we fast only so that we can, once we have finished, chew again—when do we ever feel *hunger*? It's always appetite, the desire to taste, to be diverted. Every week there is some new cracker on the market, there not so much to feed us as to entertain, more pastime than sustenance. We are, in the fullest sense, *consumers*, trained to salivate not at a bell but at the sight of a Kellogg's label or a Dunkin' Donuts box.

CAN understand the Jesus freaks turning, dope-mud-dled, to a life of self-denial and asceticism. The excesses of eighth-grade psychedelia left me feeling the same way and I turned, in 1967, to God. To the church, at least, anxious to wash away the bad aftertaste of too many Cokes and too much eyeshadow. The church I chose, the only one conceivable for a confirmed atheist, wasn't really a church at all, but a dark gray building that housed the Unitarian Fellowship. They were an earnest, liberal-mind-ed, socially-conscious congregation of thirty-five or forty. If I had been looking for spirituality, I knocked at the wrong door; the Unitarians were rationalists—scientists, mostly, whose programs would be slide shows of plant life in North Africa or discussion of migratory labor prob-lems. We believed in our fellow man.

We tried Bible reading in my Liberal Religious Youth group but in that mildewed attic room, sitting on orange crates in a circle of four, the Old Testament held no power. We gave up on Genesis and *rapped*, instead, with a casual college student who started class saying, "Man, do I have a hangover." Sometimes we sang in a choir made up of one soprano, two tenors and a tone-deaf alto, draped in shabby black robes designed for taller worshipers. After one week of singing we switched, wisely, to what Unitarians do best, to the subjects suited to orange crates. We found a Cause.

We discovered the Welfare Mothers of America—one welfare mother in particular. She was an angry, militant mother of eight (no husband in the picture) who wanted to go to the national convention in Tennessee and needed someone to foot the bill. I don't know who told us about Mrs. Mahoney, or her about us. In one excited Sunday meeting, anyway, the three of us voted to pay her way and, never having earned three dollars without spending it, never having met Peg Mahoney, we called the state office of the Unitarian Church and arranged for a two-hundred-dollar loan. Then we made lists, allocated jobs, formed committees (as well as committees can be formed, with an active membership of three, and a half dozen others who preferred to sleep in on Sundays). We would hold a spaghetti supper, all proceeds to go to the Mahoney fund.

We never heard what happened at the welfare conference—in fact, we never heard from our welfare mother again. She disappeared, with the red plaid suitcase I lent her for the journey and the new hat we saw her off in. Our two-hundred-dollar debt lingered on through not one but three spaghetti suppers, during which I discovered that there's more to Italian-style fund-raising dinners than red and white checked tablecloths and Segovia records. Every supper began with five or six helpers; as more and more customers arrived, though, fewer and fewer LRYers stayed on to help. By ten o'clock, when the last walnut-sized meat ball had been cooked and the last pot of spaghetti drained, there would be two of us left in our tomato-spotted red aprons, while all around, religious youth high on red wine sprawled and hiccuped on the kitchen floor, staggering nervously to the door every few minutes to make sure their parents weren't around. I never again felt the same about group activity—united we stand ... and that wonderful feeling I used to get at Pete Seeger concerts—singing "This Land Is Your Land"—that by working together, nothing was impossible.

After the debt was paid I left LRY, which had just discovered sensitivity training. Now the group held weekly nonverbal communication sessions, with lots of hugging and feeling that boosted attendance to triple what it had been in our old save-the-world days. It seemed that everybody's favorite topic was himself.

OUR FIRST parties were bow-tie-and-petticoat affairs on birthdays, with paint-by-number kits, gift-wrapped, for presents and little baskets of jelly beans and Indian corn for favors, and inedible white cake (eaten nonetheless) with pink or green or yellow frosting for after-party stomach-aches. Until about second grade our parties were boy-girl—we never really thought about the distinctions, the only difference between us, outside of clothing, being whether we deflated our party balloons and took them home with us (the girls) or popped them in somebody's ear (the boys).

Then, when we were seven or so, the parties segregated. It strikes me as too bad, now. It wasn't anything in *us*, but something in our surroundings that made us wary and imposed on us unnatural shame at being caught, after an especially noisy bellyflop in the town pool, with our bathing suits momentarily askew, exposing our tops (that's what we called them—the real, clinical names for things always scared us). We would have been young enough to feel natural still with boys, except that we were all in such a hurry to grow up that we affected sexy feelings and the awkwardness of crushes long before we really felt them. By second grade, at any rate, our parties were strictly all-girl or all-boy. For my friends and me, many slumber parties and little slumbering. We rolled our hair and wore our baby-doll pajamas and compared sleeping bags and told ghost stories (the vindow vasher, the pickled hand). After one slumber party, though, stories began to circulate about a certain girl who had attended it and acted "queer." Newly alerted to the existence of homosexuality, all of us imagined we saw signs of perversion wherever we turned. If you touched a friend of the same sex, by accident, you said "Excuse me"—we still do—and if it happened too often, you were a "homo" or a "queer."

Then in fifth grade, when the need for separation had perhaps become real enough, we were flung back together again, mostly by parents, into a boy-girl world. Buckled into garter belts, buttoned into suit jackets, we were deposited at the host's house at seven-thirty by our parents, who watched us file stiffly through the doors leading to his basement recreation room, two by two, like passengers aboard the ark and set afloat for the express purpose of mating. Parents would smile and poke us in the ribs and say things like "Don't come home without lipstick on your collar" (to boys—though fifth-grade girls never wore lipstick, and even if they did, would never have got it on the collar of any fifth-grade boy) or "Don't be afraid of the dark, the boys will take care of you" (chuckle). Once, at a boy-girl fifth-grade Christmas party, I remember the host's mother following me around holding a sprig of plastic mistletoe over my head and calling her son, "Look, you can kiss her" which eventually, he did. (Very few boys would have. I'm not sure if it was obedience or gallantry that made him follow through.) Afterward he looked embarrassed, but mostly just puzzled. Clearly he had imagined fireworks and dizziness and stars.

The parents at another party that I wasn't invited to, but heard about, turned out the lights themselves once everyone was settled in the father's cozy rifle- and fish-trophy-decorated den, then said "Have fun, kids," and went upstairs to watch TV. I think parents liked the cuteness of our youth, enjoyed the comedy of our fumbling. Anything in the miniature version is adorable—toy poodles, little girls dressed up in high heels with smeary lipstick, musical prodigies with half-size violins and fifth graders playing at sex, affecting the actions of their elders, without the basic needs that stirred *them* on. (Our older brothers and sisters necked at parties because they felt like necking. We did because we felt we should.) Just as the Munchkins in the *Wizard of Oz* always get a condescending smile, and so do circus midgets and anyone else who is unthreateningly small, so did we because, I think, our comic inadequacies pointed up the grown-ups' relative success. The truth is that very little went on in those first lights-out parties. Mostly we played records (Beatles, Monkees, Beach Boys, Mamas and the Papas) and ate pretzels. We usually ended up gathered around a miniature hockey set, the kind with little metal players and a plastic puck, controlled with levers on the sides, or playing a suggestive game called Twister that put us into funny positions, our legs and arms tangled, sprawled on the floor, or volleying a Ping-pong ball back and forth, using our shoes for paddles, glad to be barefoot and relieved to have something to focus our attention on besides each other.

Later, when all their prodding finally took hold and when the party games we played had progressed beyond Pass the Orange (from girl to boy to girl, holding the fruit with just your neck and chin, and letting it slide, sometimes, to your chest), the parents might have liked to call the whole thing off. By then it was too late, of course. They'd launched the ark, but when we finally set sail, beyond their placid, chaperoned harbor waters, beyond hand holding and a couple of innocent, blushing, off-target kisses on the couch, then they became suddenly surprised and indignant, and wondered how we'd gotten that way. It was no wonder, really. If you start turning the lights out in fifth grade, you're ready for something else by high school.

The diary I kept all through eighth grade dwells for whole entries—page after page after page—on a single junior high school dance. There were three each year: one in the fall, a nervous gathering more like a meeting of two warring teams than a coming together of allies; one in winter (by that time a few precocious couples had paired

up and came like newlyweds to show off before the multi-
tudes who came alone); and one in spring, the mating season when, with caution thrown to the outfield, desperate
for this one last chance before the long dull summer
ahead, we tried to find Someone to spend June with so
that, if we were going to be hot and bored, at least we
would be hot and bored together. It was this last spring
dance my diary dealt with. Not the happy recollections,
but anxious discussions of an event not yet taken place.

As secretary of the student council and chairman of decorations, it was my job to choose a theme and transform
the gym into a setting suitable for romance. (My peren-
nial role was to decorate rooms for other people to dance
in. I would do it again three years later as co-chairman of
the junior prom.) The theme of this dance was somewhat
confused—"Good Vibrations," after a song by the Beach
Boys ("She's giving me good vibrations/she's giving me
ex-ci-ta-tions . . .") combined with the idea, stolen from
the latest fad, of computer dating. For this combination
we hung streamers and dyed old sheets, and placed on a
table underneath a basketball hoop the focal point of the
evening: our computer. (Lit with Christmas tree lights,
with two slots marked "boy" and "girl," the computer was
just big enough for me to sit inside, pairing up the couples
and trying not to run my stockings.)

It was just the kind of idea that someone who didn't
dance too regularly at dances would come up with—a
guaranteed partner for everyone, a chicken in every pot.
The girls who, like me, were used to taking many trips to
the water fountain thought the computer was a great idea.
So did the boys whose agonizing job of asking someone to
dance was taken out of their hands by The Box. But for
some—red-haired Kathy and Sally, who'd been readying
herself for a career in cheerleading since sixth grade—for
them, the computer was a raw deal.

More important to me than the computer issue, though,
in 1967, was the whole question of going to the dance. It
seems odd to me now, reading in that diary, of my reluctance to ask my parents whether I could go. They would
have said yes, of course, and they would have been surprised that I even bothered to ask. But (and this is where
my fear came in) they would also have been surprised

that I wanted to go—that I, who worked so hard at being grown up and cool and analytical, would want to put myself in the sweaty hands of some skinny, slicked-down, Old Spice-y thirteen-year-old. Because, in my head, I wasn't a day under thirty-five. So when my mother asked me, "What boys do you like best?" I laughed and said they were all terrible (and so *young*) and was amazed at the openness with which some of my friends exposed their crushes. Relishing them and never, like me, ashamed.

I was ashamed of my wanting to go to the dance and of my hidden store of purple eyeshadow and inky eyeliner that I revealed the moment I emerged, after hours in the bathroom, as from a beating, with bruised-looking, shakily outlined eyes and lips so whitened with Yardley slicker that I appeared almost mouthless.

I went alone to dances. I'd come right home from school that day to wash and set my hair and put my dress on, hours early, taking *Seventeen*-model poses before the mirror, dancing in silence with the door closed, running downtown for last-minute purchases of earrings or nail polish, curling my eyelashes, as if that was all I needed— curlier lashes—to get a partner so that next time I wouldn't have to go alone. My father always offered to drive to the dance (so did my mother—she would pull up slowly to get a look at all the boys and point out the cute ones, while I sank in the seat and hoped she wouldn't kiss me good-by). Most often, though, I walked, with a scarf around my head to keep my hair from blowing and two quarters in my pocket for admission.

Once I arrived, I'd go first to the girls' room where, for a while, the absence of a boy beside me would not stand out. All of us gathered round the sinks then, to compliment dresses and hairdos and tell each other how good we looked (cute or, the ultimate compliment, *old*). We fastened garters and bra straps and hitched up slips and discussed unlikely couples and ugly dresses through the bathroom doors, almost drowned out by the sounds of water running and toilets flushing. Back in the hall, the boys were waiting, with the genial, patient looks of resignation (Women! What can you expect?...) that must have been learned from their fathers. They'd meet their dates at the bathroom door (the ones who came with girls) and escort them into the gym, one hand touching her back—not clasped around her shoulder, usually, not that until high school—just touching, palm flat, to indicate staked-out territory. Hands were always a problem that way—they hung and swung and dangled and sweated, and nothing that you did with them seemed right, not crossing them (too tough) or putting them on your hips (too I-dare-you), or making tight, tense fists or letting the fingers hang loose at your sides. Few of us, dancing, felt really graceful or free, the way dancing was supposed to make you feel. We were too conscious of feet and hips and hair and dresses and ties and braces and, most of all, hands.

We sat in rows along the gym wall, boys on one side, girls on the other, dancers in between and the group (two guitars, a drum, a tambourine, or just a record player) on the stage at the front of the room, with knots of mostly girls gathered to watch, happy—or at least less miserable than otherwise—to have something to focus their eyes on. Eyes, like hands, were a problem. Meeting someone else's was scary; looking away—like playing chicken in a hot rod (who brakes first?)—seemed cowardly, but looking too long was proof of interest, and left you open to be hurt. So the girls looked mostly at the safe things—couples dancing, chaperones smiling benignly on the few who kissed, the flag, the DRINK MILK poster on the wall, the crepe-paper streamers and balloons. (The boys would pop them when the dance was over, reverting suddenly, like Cinderella as the clock struck twelve, to childhood birthday parties.)

I can't remember now how I spent all those hours on my metal folding chair not dancing, or why I came back, dance after dance, once I'd seen how it was to be. Sometimes an unattached boy would come toward me, and I'd rise to dance (hoping to save him the agony of an invitation—"Wanna dance?" or, more likely, just a shrug to indicate that there was nothing better to do) and then, once I was standing, I'd discover that it wasn't me at all he was after, so I'd keep moving, barely changing course, toward the water fountain, as if all I'd wanted was a good stiff drink of water. Sometimes I'd dance with another girl (giggling loudly, just so everyone would know we were only doing it for fun, that we weren't—dreaded term—

queer). Or, toward the end, and desperate, needing some names to tell my mother when she asked me who I danced with (and never able, quite, to lie) I'd ask a boy to dance. Never someone I really liked, but someone safe and sexless who would know, in case the faces I made, as I danced with him, didn't make it plain enough, that all I wanted was someone—anyone—in pants, who'd give me an excuse for dancing. (Dancing in front of someone else I *did* like, hoping he'd notice.)

At every dance there would be two or three boys I could count on to ask me, boys who danced with every girl's-room-and-water-fountain type—the wallflowers—but far from being grateful to them for saving us from sitting wondering where to put our hands and on what to focus our eyes, we hated them, stuck out our tongues as we leaned our heads on their sloping shoulders in a slow dance, fast-danced so far apart we hoped no one could tell who our partner was. We'd run back to our seats and our girl friends the very second the last note was played (not lingering a second on the dance floor, as most couples did), making a big thing of washing our hands afterward, if he had touched us. When I came home, though, and met my mother at the door, asking whom I'd danced with, it was those boys' names I'd use, and multiply, to manufacture a good, popular-sounding answer. She asks me now why I lied about the fun I had at dances, and I'm not sure of the answer. I think the reason is that none of us wants to appear pathetic, no one wants to be seen as a loser, and my only hope of winning was to pretend that I'd already won.

All of us in eighth grade knew that Sue loved Bob and vice versa. (All but me, at least. From the beginning, as I reminded my more romantic friends later, when it was all over, I had been suspicious.) Sue and Bob were no older than the rest of us—fourteen—but the permanence of their situation made them seem to us at least sixteen. As early as October, Bob had signed Sue up to go with him to every dance that year, plus the big freshman dance the next fall. She wore his ring, with tape wound around the band to keep it on her finger, and he wore on his wrist a shackle-like silver chain with a name tag on it that read SUE.

All through the school day they passed notes to each other—mushy, romantic, badly spelled descriptions of how much they missed each other, signed with half a page of "love's" on Bob's part, calmer, more domestic plans for the future written by Sue, with "Love ya" at the bottom. Sue and Bob weren't in all the same classes that year, so helpful friends—proud to be caught up in the drama—delivered notes from one room to the other, using their student council or office helper status to get them through the halls and claiming, always, to have a message for Sue from the nurse, or a note for Bob from the principal. A couple of the teachers knew what was up, but they must have thought it was cute (the way kids playing grown-up always are) because they never interfered. In the process of delivery the contents of the notes tended to lose a certain privacy, to spill all over the place, in fact. Sue and Bob's correspondence abounded with passionate confidences and arrows pointing to blank spaces with captions that read "This is where I kissed the envelope." And there were other enviably soppy exchanges, which Bob, at his receiving end, would stuff into his pants pocket while Sue put hers into that pregnant purse which hung from her shoulder or on the back of her chair during classes. (We stole it sometimes, just to scare her.)

Aside from the note passing, though, their relationship seemed tame. They were the old married couple of the eighth grade, more like chaperones at dances than like kids. They kissed sometimes while dancing, but mostly they just held hands, as if they had already explored each other so well that nothing else was needed. Sue often resembled a tired, not-tonight-honey housewife with Bob, already dreaming, as they held hands in the corner while the newer, younger couples danced, of a ring and a house and a kitchen and a baby. All the romantics of the junior high were positive they would get married. (We shivered at how close that put us to being grown up, trying out Mrs. with our names, and matching them with different boys' last names. "Just think" we'd whisper to each other, "nine months from now I could be a *mother*.") That notion scared and thrilled us, and it must have terrified the boys.

In the middle of some make-out party embrace, drunk with Sue's hooks and fasteners, Bob must have agreed to anything she said, but sometimes, in the brighter hours, he looked a little wistful as he passed the boys out on the playground playing soccer and leaning into the engines of the older kids' cars, while he was surely headed for a station wagon.

He strayed once, with someone's visiting cousin, and Sue heard about it. Like the wife of an adulterous husband, she talked it over with her friends and decided at last to forgive him, but Bob had discovered he didn't want to be forgiven so, at the end of junior high, the first real romance of our class broke up. The ring went back, the bracelet disappeared, Bob was a bachelor again, and almost giddy with his freedom, while Sue moved through the halls like a divorcée. No one would make her mistakes again. Couples would take themselves seriously, but only because love was a necessary delusion, no longer quite so sacred. It was a word from a dozen songs, the rhyme to "dove" and "above," and changing as fashions and the week's top ten. We entered high school believing in it less, and ready for the soap opera to begin.

Make-up and high heels, or being allowed to stay out till midnight, or a ten-dollar allowance were not, for us, the indications that we'd grown up. Even little kids were getting those things by the time we came along. But we knew we'd grown up on the day we got our driver's licenses.

I'd planned for mine since I was twelve, imagining the shopping trips I'd make; the red convertible I'd buy. Even after I got my license, of course, those things didn't come. (Too much traffic for city-shopping driving; too little money for convertibles.) But even without them, and with my parents' reminder every time I left in the car to buckle my seat belt and drive carefully, my sense of release at having that slip of paper—my license—in the glove compartment was tremendous. Not that I'd ever been a tightly disciplined prisoner in our house, but any time I had to go somewhere too far for biking, it meant asking someone to drive me. I had to have a place to go to and a certain time when I'd be coming back. Besides, my parents drove

like senior citizens. I felt embarrassed when kids from
school roared past and saw me in our hulking Oldsmo-
bile—we never passed or drove, like in the movies, with
only one hand on the wheel, and never played the radio.
(My mother said she needed all her concentration for the
road. I said, then how can you drive and breathe at the
same time, and she said, listen, do you want to walk?)
Once I had my license I could do all those things—cruise
with no real destination, honk the horn when I passed a
friend, flirt with the tail of our car and the blinker lights
when someone I knew pulled up behind me. My bicycle
went into the garage.

When I was sixteen I got just a license. Some boys got
cars too—pointy-finned Chevys and Volkswagens covered
with flags and peace signs, chrome-portholed Buicks that
they took jobs to support, as they'd support a wife, and
rattling, rubber-laying Fords painted dull black so if the
cops came after them for speeding they could hide in the
bushes without the gleam of lights on paint to give them
and their cars away. There was a yellow Model-T with a
rumble seat and an old black Model-A, less flashy, more
respected, with a window-shade in back and a motor that
balked at hills. Cars and their drivers often merged for us,
so that late at night, lying in bed, I'd know when Paul, the
owner of the Model-A, came by. And stretched out on the
lawn on summer evenings when just a flash of blue and
white drove past (a grafting job—white door transplanted
on a body that was blue) I knew it must be Harvey, going
to buy beer with Rich.

And when we got our licenses, of course, our parents
stopped driving us to parties. We drove ourselves, or rode
in cars driven by friends or boy friends. Fast, on the way
there, faster—accelerator foot beer-loosened—on the way
home. "Don't ride with him if he's drunk," our parents
would tell us, "we'll come and pick you up," but that was
an unthinkable idea; visions of a cautious station wagon
and a father in his bathrobe, bent over the wheel, his
headlights beaming over a path of beer cans and parked
cars with the shadows of heads and arms and hands
showing against the back seat, and coming out to meet
him, with a mouthful of toothpaste or peppermints and all

the neat curls he'd admired, hours before, all of them suspiciously tangled now. . . .

Toward the end of my high school career, there was marijuana, but mostly it was Budweiser, picked up by a mature-looking nineteen-year-old with an altered driver's license, or got by standing next to the supermarket door and waiting for someone to come in who was old enough to buy for us, and not too old *not* to buy. The boys who hovered in the shadows, leaning on the Coke machine, would look over every customer, and when they saw a likely one they'd mumble the password, like something out of a prohibition movie—"Buy?" and if the twenty-one-year-old agreed, they'd hand over our pooled allowances and make arrangements for a rendezvous where they could pick the stuff up.

Arrangements always seemed to me ridiculously elaborate, complicated not so much for the sake of the town cops who, in our imaginations, spent their lives tracking us for signs of liquor, but because the complex beer pick-up system we had was fun, a combination treasure hunt and spy game. At half a dozen spots along some country road we'd stop and burrow in the snow for a case someone had planted a few hours before—digging unsuccessfully, sometimes, when the markers we had left had disappeared, and, once, coming on a case that wasn't ours. Driving with a hot back seat of frozen beer, we were all paranoid, imagining sirens and blue lights, unmarked cars. We had tricks, though—watching telephone wires for the reflection of light that indicated an oncoming car (so that we'd lower our cans in time), thick parkas with a hundred pockets in the lining and the sleeves even. (The boys who wore them, can and bottle stuffed, entered the party houses like frozen-jointed soldiers.) And sometimes we'd buy a keg and let the beer spill from the tap like water, with—after all the effort we'd spent in getting it—a wonderful, reckless feeling of abundance.

When a new car appeared in the school parking lot, a bunch of boys would go and check it out, the owner standing by and leaning, casual and proud, against the hood, hoping they'd notice, but not pointing out, the wire-wheel hub caps and the leather seats. Beside them in the parking lot, more familiar, already inspected and broken in, other cars were lined up, warming in the sun. Couples, at lunch, would go and sit in them, chewing their sandwiches side by side, facing straight ahead, as if the Oyster River parking lot were a drive-in movie just about to start. Familiar silhouette: a boy's head, (his neck almost army-stiff) and, on his shoulder, the head of a girl, with his hand resting on her hair—motionless, often—while they contemplated asphalt and dashboard.

Cars weren't just for driving, of course, they were for parking. There was often no place else to go, and so—like weary nomads (absurdly, the image of Mary and Joseph being turned away at the inn comes to mind) high school couples found refuge in their cars. Maybe that's why cars held so much importance—why sometimes they'd be ritually passed on from graduating senior to up-and-coming junior boy—so much had taken place inside them, so much drunk and explored.

Even now, a couple of years removed from beer and bucket seats and gear shifts sticking up at awkward angles and late night radios glowing in the dark until, at last, the announcer would speak of "this morning," not "tonight"—even now I feel uneasy, writing about what went on in those cars. It was a pretty important thing to do (I catch myself from saying *pastime*—it was more central than that. It's hard not slipping into anthropologist talk, tribal life among the high school natives—there is a tendency to condescend). Observing seems like an intrusion, because it's easy to find comedy in zealous awkwardness, easy to smile (safe in one's composed delicacy and arranged grace—ankles crossed and hair brushed) at the clumsiness of others. The truth is that what went on in the seats of cars, on rec. room couches and summer cabin mattresses—stiff with December ice and warmed with no more than a blanket and a body—those things weren't meant to be watched.

And yet nobody minded being seen. It was a shock, when I first realized that, the year I turned fourteen and acted in a high school summer theater. The cast held parties every night—rehearsal parties, set-building parties, parties because the play was over and parties to celebrate the parties. I was just about the youngest one there, the most inexperienced, certainly, and looked away, gasping "excuse me" the first time I walked into a room and found a couple kissing horizontally. But turning my head was no help; wherever I looked there was a boy biting a girl's ear or a girl rubbing a boy's back while he rubbed hers, from inside her shirt, or two people kissing in a way I'd never seen before—not lovely and romantic, the way movie stars kissed (that's all changed now too, of course) but what I and my still-uninitiated friends called "wet kissing," as if they were eating overripe nectarines. And once, in great relief, I saw a vacant couch to sit on—a corner I could look in without blushing—and found myself on top of someone's body, under a blanket. I learned that summer that no one cared what I saw, as they emerged from under the blankets, puffy-eyed and tousled; no one felt awkward facing me (as I had felt sure they would, now that I knew what they did) after it was all over.

There were lots of parties from then on, and rumors of goings-on at movies and dances, but I think ninth grade was when our attitudes really changed, when we stopped being shocked, embarrassed voyeurs to whom sex still seemed, most of all, dirty. That spring our English class made a field trip to the city to see *Romeo and Juliet* performed. The bus ride down was pretty much the same as bus trips since first grade—singing "99 Bottles of Beer on the Wall" (all the way down to one), lots of seat-changing and flouncing up and down the aisles, calling the roll, hanging out windows ("Hey, mister, did anybody ever tell you you look like Paul Newman? Well, you don't"). But on the trip back, softened by the tragedy of young love divided, our stomachs too full of hotdogs and Howard Johnson sundaes for singing, and vaguely carsick, a change took place. Girls had always sat with girls and boys with boys, mixing only to make wisecracks. Halfway home though, Margie, queen of our class from the first grade on, switched seats so she could sit with Buzzy, JV (junior varsity) basketball star, the one we girls loved best of all. Word traveled even to the front that they were holding hands, that they had slid down in the seat, and finally that they were kissing. No one dared turn around to look. Sixty minutes later we pulled in to the high school parking lot and our own Romeo and Juliet emerged—Buzzy to draw his hand across his lips and grin, then to pull the comb from his back pocket and run through his hair, Margie to smooth her skirts and move off to the girls' room followed by the rest of us, who scrubbed our hands for surely ten minutes while she told us what he'd done, crying finally and saying did we think she was *fast* and oh, now no one would *respect* her. But respect no longer mattered so much—the Snow White, fairy princess, only-other-people-do-it image had died and been replaced by something else. Now—far from concealing what we had and were ashamed of, we'd make the most of it.

THE DAY we entered high school, we got a long talk from the principal, telling us what a great group we were, and what a great school this was, and another from the vice principal, telling us that he was fair, but, buddy, not to cross him (anticipating already what an ungreat group we were), and still another talk from the guidance counselor, who, anybody with a problem would soon discover, was *not* a counselor, and would have been surprised, to say the least, if we had come to him with what the nurse called "personal problems"—those were for your clergyman or your doctor. What the guidance counselor did, and would repeat each fall, with only slight alterations, for our sophomore, junior and senior pep talks, was to hold up a blank sheet of paper and, after a long pause he must have learned from TV aspirin commercials, tell us that the blank sheet represented our record so far, "a clean bill of goods, like they say." And four (or three, two, one years later) when we entered college, it would be filled. What we did now would determine whether we'd enter college or not, and we all had a chance, a fresh start, a whole new ball game.

It was a good feeling, I suppose, the idea that the slate was really blank, except that of course in a variety of important ways it wasn't. Our junior high school reputations followed us—old rumors surfaced again, dislikes and friendships remained. Like biology lab planarians who, when their heads or tails are cut off, sprout new ones like the ones they lost, we were already trapped, with a set of junior high school genes that reasserted themselves at our ninth-grade rebirth. What we wore and who our friends were, and what positions in the school our older brothers and sisters had held all determined what slot would be waiting for us. Only a new kid coming in might write his own ticket, but then he'd have to work, to flaunt his credentials without seeming to, and there would be a test, out on the basketball court—or, a subtler one for girls, constant surveillance in the halls, our watching her clothes and hair and how she held her books and what she said to boys who came and swung on her locker door to talk. I could have told, on that first day, sitting in the bleachers and knowing better than to be hopeful, who would be valedictorian and who would score the baskets and who would crash his car and who would end up pregnant—our records weren't so blank after all.

In spite of the sense of fatalism, there was an awesome push, from the first, toward college—"the college of your choice." Those spaces on our application blanks and records left for "extracurricular activities" loomed large when we joined clubs and committees, and threatened us (we visualized a huge black pen filling them in) each time we were discovered skipping gym or trading homework papers. The unfilled-in white sheet, growing steadily grayer, hovered like a ghost.

So did the SAT exams and the achievement tests, the miles of fill-in-the-blanks and vocabulary words and analogies ahead, the nightmare moment when you realize you filled in the number-one answer in the number-two blank, and number two in three . . . all the way through one hundred, with two minutes left before the bell. The practice file cards of vocabulary words that didn't do much good (I could never remember *halcyon*, though it came up every time), the nervous sleep the night before, the superstitious rituals, the sheath of sharpened number-two pencils (the poorest students always carried the most, as if pencils were arrows and the one with the most had the best chance for a bull's eye). When it was over (sometimes we'd sit through six hours' worth of tests) we'd gather outside the door, unable, after so long a stretch of testing, to leave it behind, lingering over the questions, reconstructing math problems and comparing answers, with some one-pencil carrier modestly demonstrating what we'd done wrong. And finally, months later, getting our scores back and comparing them, taking the College Entrance Exam Board's word, above our own, for who we were. We exchanged scores, all of us who'd done well, and acted disappointed that we'd done so *terribly*. We were card players waiting to see what sort of hands the competition had before laying down our own. And then, like the dissembling show-offs we were, like slim girls who count calories and moan that they've got to start dieting, in front of fat ones eating chocolate bars, we'd murmur "730—*how awful!*" in earshot of those who got 500s and who, with a humility we might well have envied, if we'd had the sense, simply tucked their scores away, relegated to the state university, and resigned to it.

Doing poorly on an achievement test was bad enough, but there at least you could blame it on not studying, on not "living up to your potential." But a mediocre aptitude score was devastating; a score of 540 had to mean that 540 ran in your veins and in your chromosomes, and no matter what you did, you couldn't change it, so you might as well not try.

And when the whole college push was over, the tests studied for and taken, the scores in, the teacher recommendations and the questions filled out ("The most valuable experience in my life ..." "If I were going to write a book ..."), when the last campus tour and college interview was over—a firm handshake, to show energy; look-him-in-the-eye, for honesty and straightforwardness; a calm, unhysterical laugh to show a good sense of humor, and a conservative-length skirt to show that what you're interested in isn't the boys—when all that was over I discovered the final irony, not just for me, but for many: that getting into college no longer mattered as it used to. If I got in I'd go, and if I didn't, I'd go out into what prep school kids call the real world (I imagined myself at some Iowa truck stop, sizzling cheeseburgers, talking straight and gutsy with truck driver sages). For the first time, some of us began to examine the Diploma Mystique—the fact of life we'd never thought to question, that *of course* you finish high school and of course you go to college and choose a major and graduate, and if you don't go on to graduate school, you get a job. School and education had little to do with each other, often enough—we knew that. More and more, though, it was *education* that we cared about, and a kind of pure knowledge that sometimes seemed unrelated to what went on at college. "A" students, honor roll types I knew, dropped out of high school in their senior year to study on their own, college-prepped private school boys graduated and went off to learn automobile mechanics or to apprentice with carpenters, or to farm.

What changed quite suddenly, I think, was (it must sound hopelessly large and generalized) our whole set of values. Not all of us, by any means, but a great many at the end of the sixties turned away from the old goals, the old definitions of success and happiness. I found it in myself—a lightning-bolt kind of revelation that I'd never really asked myself whether a college degree was what I wanted. Or, more precisely, I'd never considered that I might *not* want one. College was presented to us as a not-necessarily-accessible, but naturally desirable goal, long before the ninth-grade, college-of-your-choice speech, and long after. The fact that college is not right for everyone—not just because they can't get in or because they want business school instead—seems pretty obvious, but it's a neglected fact, I think.

Everything from high school on splits down the middle on the college or non-college issue, and it determines the courses you take and the friends you have, and when you're likely to get married and what your chances of getting shot in some war are. Kids my age are college snobs, identifying themselves, at parties, by the school they go to, especially if it's a name with ivy on it. People who would never dream of announcing "Hello, I'm very bright. How smart are you?" will wait for any opening (kidding themselves that the admission has a certain aptness) to say "I go to Harvard. Where do you go?" which comes down to the same thing. The ones who don't go to college are understandably resentful of the split. (I've learned, from hitchhiking, never to identify myself to beat-up Chevy drivers as a student. I am a secretary, or a waitress, and we stay friendly.) In spite of scholarships and minority recruiting, college campuses are, to many, the territory of the enemy. It makes for political and social divisions, and it perpetuates itself down through the generations. Often the children of non-college-goers will be raised with the unquestioned assumption that college is not for them, (just as I grew up, unquestioning, that college *was* for me). They will be classed, early in school, as "underachievers" and trained accordingly, advised to take shop and home economics courses, categorized by other students and by teachers and finally by each other, and their underachieving will often have lots more to do with what's expected (or not expected) of them than with what they can really do. To them, the talk of fresh starts and an equal chance for all at getting into college must sound pretty funny.

A MOVIE of the Monterrey Pop Music Festival came out in 1967. The first song they played was "If You're Going to San Francisco" ("Be sure to wear some flowers in your hair ... cause summertime will be a love-in there ..."). The music was soft, almost music-box pretty, with lots of harmonies and gentle guitars. And what they meant by love-in (the word has disappeared now) were the tame, Sunday-in-the-park-type gatherings with lots of kites and balloons and bubble blowing and marijuana. We called it pot, and wore buttons—the brave ones, the really way-out types, at least—that said "this country's going to pot." Drugs, back then, meant marijuana still. Heroin and cocaine were for thin, red-eyed unshaven men with switchblades in their pockets, not love children with flowers in their hair.

The faces in the crowd at Monterrey—even the older ones—seem young to me now. I feel, looking at their unaged faces, the way I feel looking at pictures of President Kennedy hours before he was shot, or Hiroshima just before the bomb—the feeling that something could have been prevented if only they'd known what was coming. I feel now, watching that movie again, like someone standing on a mountain top looking down to a pair of eager, unaware climbers and, at the same moment, seeing an avalanche roaring toward them. The hipness of their dress lay still in the accessories (boys in Brooks Brothers shirts with beads around the necks; girls in fashion magazine lipstick and love beads). There was a basic squareness still about that gathering in '67—small departures from tradition while remaining still within the set of never-questioned structures that were common then. The audience at Monterrey sat on chairs, not blankets, and clapped at the ends of songs because no other form of applause had been invented yet. The idea of questioning the established forms had yet to arise. That's what explains how such an enormous step—from Monterrey to Woodstock, just two years later—could take place so easily. The distance between sitting in concertgoing clothes or folding chairs and rolling naked in the mud is not as far as it may seem. Only the first move—the suspension of the established taken-for-granted structures of life is hard. Once they're gone, once the first garter is shyly unfastened, the rest of the striptease comes easily.

I did not go to Woodstock. But like everyone who was about my age the summer it happened, I followed the festival all through the crowded, rainy days while it lasted, and when it was over, I listened to the kids who'd been there as they straggled home. Over and over again, the same facts proudly reported: that Woodstock was, during the festival, the second largest city in New York, more peaceable than any other of its size. We goaded each other on, feeding cues like members of a comedy act ("Tell about the time when everybody slid in the mud." "What was it like when Hendrix played?"), because, like countlessly repeated bedtime stories from childhood the Woodstock mythology appealed to us for its familiarity, and for something else too—the notion that a bunch of kids had pulled something like that off so successfully. We were a group who had little to be proud of—no real youth spokesman, no youth painters, youth writers. Our artists had to be musicians—who were successful not in spite of their age, but because of it, which is why we loved them. They spoke for the accomplishment of a spokesman-less group with little else to show for its existence on the earth. Our war protests seemed to us impotent; we had always been regarded in terms of a consumer bloc, good for nothing more than buying records and acne medications. Now at last we'd found something else, seen how many of us there were ("You can't imagine how big the crowd was," a friend told me, "all people like us"). It was a false and misleading sense of kinship Woodstock gave us—a password that included anyone who'd been there, seen the movie or bought the record—but it gave us a sense of our own power, and a pride we needed right about then. Today, several years later, kids meeting each other will bring up Woodstock still and, finding that they were both there, will greet like old fraternity brothers. Theirs is the joy that aging basketball stars get when they meet someone who knew them in their glory—the day they scored the winning points, in overtime, from the center of the court with three seconds left to play.

1969

In my junior year I had English and algebra and French and art and history, but what I really had was fun. It was a year when I didn't give thought to welfare mothers or war or peace or brotherhood; the big questions in my life were whether to cut my hair and what the theme of the junior prom should be. (I left my hair long. We decided on a castle.) Looking back on a year of sitting around just talking and drinking beer and driving around drinking beer and dancing and drinking beer and just drinking beer, I can say "Ah yes, the post-Woodstock disenchantment; the post-Chicago, post-election apathy; the rootlessness of a generation whose leaders had all been killed . . ." But if that's what it was, we certainly didn't know it. Our lives were dominated by parties and pranks and dances and soccer games. (We won the state championship that year. Riding home in a streamer-trailing yellow bus, cheering "We're Number One," it never occurred to us that so were forty-nine other schools in forty-nine other states.) It was a time straight out of the goldfish-swallowing fifties, with a difference. We knew just enough to feel guilty, like trick or treaters nervously passing a ghost with a UNICEF box in his hand. We didn't feel bad enough not to build a twenty-foot cardboard- and crepe-paper castle, but we knew enough to realize, as we ripped it down the next morning, Grecian curls unwinding limply down our backs, that silver painted cardboard and tissue paper carnations weren't biodegradable.

HIGH SCHOOL yearbooks list club memberships, not grades. Which makes sense because what is remembered, looking back, are hardly ever classes and books read but social events, what guidance counselors refer to as "extracurricular activities." If you aren't a part of class meetings and outing clubs and Latin banquets (we used to cut up sheets each year, parading in our permanent press togas) then it is the very absence of those things—and not the major themes in *Silas Marner*—that you'll think of when you remember high school. My school was full of clubs—the outing club (we drank beer and planned trips that we never took); the pep club, math club, art club, dance club and lots of others—never named or listed in the yearbook, but just as tightly knit and clubbish—the "hippies" (they passed each other bags of chalk dust while the shocked "straights" whispered they were taking opium); the hoods, whose cars seemed always to need tinkering; the cute, the beautiful, the cool, the popular. If anybody doubted who was who, they had only to look up at the lobby wall where every April (Junior Prom time) the names of all the couples who were going were taped up. For some it was announcement of victory, and they will never have so fine a time, be so *on top,* again.

At Oyster River, the accomplishments of the debating team went almost unnoticed. There were just four on the team and the debate coach, their file boxes and attaché cases filled with blank paper and sharpened pencils for the scribbling down of points they rarely had rebuttals for. Their wins and, mostly, their losses went unannounced at Oyster River—the team brought no glory, no drama, no violence. The math team did a little better. The manipulation of numbers is maybe a more manly pastime, closer to sport. But even math failed to excite our student body. At our school it was sports that mattered.

We didn't play football. The parents in a university town are too concerned with brains and concussions for that, perhaps. Our boys (we thought of them possessively as ours, although I never dared lay claim to them myself) were never as burly as those from the nearby factory towns. There was a casual, compact, debonair quality about them—even when sweating—that suited soccer.

I followed all the games from bake sale tables, selling popcorn to support a prom I doubted I'd attend, watching the players less than their cheerleader girl friends whose prom thrones and rose arbors, I reflected bitterly, my popcorn and my brownies would be financing. I disliked cheerleaders on principle because they spent so much time on what had always seemed to me (a scholar-TV watcher) a meaningless activity; because they were always getting out of English early and riding the team bus to away games, because they spent their idle moments in classes going over cheers under their breath, doing little tap dances under their desks; because their hair was always blond and their noses always turned up and their voices always smart enough to sound lovably dumb—but of course what I really held against cheerleaders was the fact that I wasn't one of them.

While the sustaining spirit of the cheering squad depended most of all on jealousy and bitchiness (it seemed to me), with every girl cartwheeling for herself, each one trying to kick and flip higher than the one before with what, to me, was depressing *perkiness,* the team itself—the soccer boys—seemed really to be composed of friends, dribbling and passing to each other; sprawling in the mud and patting bottoms (the cheerleaders wiggled theirs) in a brotherly spirit their fans along the side lines never matched. School spirit that we heard so much about meant yelling things like "Kill him" "Cream them" "Smash them" and, when we failed to kill, "You bastard."

And that was what was cultivated. Every morning, after a game, our principal would read the soccer scores over the PA system ("Oyster River 8, Farmington *Zilch*") with a gusto he could never muster for debate and math. Then, before the big, end-of-fall championship, there'd be a compulsory pep rally held in the gym, with a speech from the coach and a big hand for all "our boys" and a recap of the season's highlights, which meant every play of every game, and a pentecostal-style audience-participation cheer, beginning with "Who's the greatest team?" led by the principal. And we'd scream "Bobcats" back, in answer. "Who's Number One?" "Bobcats!" "What did you say?" "Bobcats!" "LOUDER!" "BOBCATS!"

And then, of course, the cheerleaders would lead a cheer, spotless in white and blue, proclaiming our team to be "Rrrrred HOT," while the boys themselves stood by examining their sneakers, looking mostly pink. Some of us tried to escape the rallies, hiding in bathrooms or ducking out side doors and going home, but there were always teachers on patrol to catch us, and the penalties for poor school spirit were stiff ones, so we rarely tried to get away. The school hippies openly yawned or made up their own cheers, lounging on the bleachers in happy groups. For me it wasn't so much a matter of deep conviction that I couldn't cheer (I liked soccer); I simply couldn't shout out "Bobcats," I guess because cheering reduced my value to that of just another mouth, another set of vocal chords, another bandwagon-jumper. To some—the ones who cheered so happily—it was, I guess, a pleasure to feel part of a huge and seemingly united crowd—assimilated. But not everyone was as confident and comfortable as they looked, I suspect. (Sometimes safety comes not out of silence but from making noise.) Many others may, like me, have mouthed the words and tossed their jelly beans out of the bus window the next day, riding home victori-

ous, from The Biggest Game of all, not out of true aban-
donment but out of the desire to look that way.

Almost every high school drama club I know of has a
Green Room backstage. It may not be green, and it may
not even be much of a room (a closet, a loft, a corner by
the fire escape) but there will be someplace where The
Drama People sit, not just during plays and rehearsals, but
between plays too (we called them "Shows"—very Broad-
way, we were) and during lunch hours and study halls and
skipped classes. They come—members of the drama club,
and I was one—to play cards and to talk plays and past,
relived glories, quoting lines from old productions of *Tea-
house of the August Moon* and *Harvey*, with lots of *in*
jokes. They give to costumes and to the set attention that
their classes never arouse; they play with the lighting and
bristle when someone who isn't Drama Club comes near
it; they hang lights, sending messages back and forth on
walkie-talkies, though they're standing barely fifteen feet
apart.

And except for an occasional dark horse discovery—
fresh talent, *new blood*—they get all the parts in all the
plays. Rarely, one or two may have some flair, but most
of them have picked up what they know from plays on
"Hallmark Hall of Fame" and from the high school English teacher who directs them, and teaches them how to
fall on stage, and how to put on spirit gum, and how to sit
down like a little old man. (Loosen your trousers first,
then lower slowly, putting your hand on the chair seat first
to indicate unsteadiness. We worked it into every play.)
Each one has his specialty: there is the perpetual ingénue,
who must have been told once that she looked cute when
she bit her lip and has been doing it ever since; the English
accent specialist, the boy who kisses well onstage and the
ham, who all the people in the audience think has great
talent ("Straight to Hollywood, kid," they inscribe in his
yearbook). A great ad libber, he has been known to
change the whole ending of a play—his Macduff forgot
about the "from his mother's womb/Untimely ripp'd"
business, but no one cared because he made such funny
faces when he carried Macbeth's head onstage.

Something about amateur dramatics invites cliquishness.

It's the roar-of-the-grease-paint, on-with-the-show, break-a-leg glitter that even the treading of our high school's squeaky boards and the rising of our mothy velvet curtain gave us—"show biz." Acting was, for the uncreative, an entree to the arts, for the show-off a legitimate excuse to do just that, a chance to be looked at and listened to by everyone. You can't fake being a musician; you may fake talent, but either you know how to make notes come from the instrument or you don't. There's no short cut to the discipline that comes from hours of playing scales or, for a dancer, working at the barre, but anyone can learn a line, step on a stage, project his voice and call himself an actor. Without self-discipline or training or talent, amateur actors fall in love with the intoxicating sound of applause and the idea that they are dashing, exciting, colorful people, instead of potential outcasts who have found a niche, not in the obscure corners of the school, but on center stage.

The desire to be thin began to haunt the girls of my generation. We were not the only ones who counted calories, of course, but we are specially prone to the obsession, caring not so much about figure as about flatness. Never really aware of Marilyn Monroe (she died when we were nine; we knew her best from an Andy Warhol silk screen), our models came from the ironing board school—large eyed, elbow-jutting girls in *Seventeen* and, of course, Twiggy. It's as if we rejected growing up and sought, with flat chests and hips narrow enough to slip through a porthole, to keep forever young—pre-teen, in fact, frozen in a time when life (as we remember it at least) seemed simpler. Maybe they still seek curves and cleavages in the Midwest and South, where a teen-ager's perfect weight stands at a full ten pounds beyond the Eastern and Pacific ideal, but in New York the girl who blossoms early mourns her ripeness and looks enviously at the lucky ones whose bikini tops fit better on the back—those starving-orphan shoulder blades—than on the front.

Current fashion dictates a thin image or, maybe, the thin image dictates current fashion. Purple tights are meant for spindle legs; boys' sleeveless undershirts are embroidered for girls who want to look like boys—girls with sad eyes and trembling lips who dress and move and talk, in this era of de-masking, T-grouping, group-groping, with what's become a favorite noun, the highest compliment—vulnerability. The plastic wrappings and metallic layers we sported in the sixties have disappeared along with heavy, masking make-up and stiff lacquered hairdos sculptured from a night in jumbo rollers.

And flesh, once the sign of a generous, passionate soul, is now a kind of mask itself—a sign of unecological wastefulness, consumerism, undisciplined living. From love-of-flesh we've come to love-of-bone, to the striving for bodies that mirror our tastes in books (Zen) and foods (health) and clothes (artfully drab and down-home) and occupations (the austere life—farming) and people. On all sides we're bombarded with reinforcements of our thin ideal—in store windows and movies and magazines that cannot go a month without some exercise or diet, magazines that fill their pages with before-and-after tales of former fatness and with send-away-for sauna pants and strange-looking "mummy wraps" that let you sweat away an unwise ice cream cone.

And here are the teen-age girls, hopping on and off their scales three times daily holding in their breath to hold in their stomachs, weighing bird-sized scoops of cottage cheese to reach a size still smaller, agonizing over a gained pound ("I can't believe it! I'm up to ninety-nine!") and fasting to an almost hallucinatory high—all for that glorious moment when someone says "Honey, you look just awful, you're so thin," at which point they know they're *almost* thin enough. Sometimes they try to sleep the weight off, or stick a finger down their throats to purge their stomachs of an extra bowl of yoghurt. They talk endlessly of diets about to be embarked on (like trips, with every day's itinerary mapped out, except this is a tour of sights *not* seen, foods *not* eaten) and tally calories and carbohydrate counts with a skill that somehow disappears during math exams. They think more about food than the people who still eat, but they cherish an image of themselves as disregarding food altogether. Eating is a masculine pastime; it's daintier to refuse food than to take it, and more feminine to sip unflavored gelatin than to bite a hamburger. The Scarlett O'Hara who ate before the picnic so that she wouldn't gorge herself in front of her beaux is not dead yet.

Still, there's something absolutely contemporary about The Diet: the idea that you can accomplish change—transformation—not by anything you do (for we are an often lethargic group) but by the thing you *don't* do—that is, eating. I think of the cafeteria table where I sat and didn't eat lunch all through my junior year—an all-girl table of constant dieters who would inform us of the calorie count of every item that appeared on the table moments before it disappeared into someone's mouth. "Carrot stick—fifteen calories!" some helpful friend would announce. "Oh no," someone would say, "you're forgetting the energy you burn up chewing. It's actually —2."

We should all have been telephone poles, but there were those after-school Cokes downtown (like something out of Judy Garland-Mickey Rooney, with a jukebox soundtrack) to make up for the dieting. And bake sales. Every Saturday, just about, some club would be raising money with a card table full of brownies set up beside the drugstore. Sometimes there would be a car wash instead, but car washes called for boys, and the boys weren't much for fund-raising. It was the girls—the women behind the men—who ran our school, the smart cheerleaders who made their big, grinning boy friends think they were thinking. And it was the girls who baked the chocolate-chip cookies that sent the Outing Club canoeing, the shortbread for somebody's open-heart surgery (we loved to rally for a cause; valentine hearts or real ones—it hardly mattered). It was the girls who kneaded the bread dough—often the very ones who were the most dedicated dieters—that paid for the prom decorations only girls would notice anyway, and the girls, some of them, who baked even though they'd never get nearer to the prom than clean-up day the morning after. But somehow kneading that bread and selling it brought them closer to the event, so they spent on their banana breads and their German tortes what they would have put into eye make-up and Grecian curls.

Anyway, we'd all write these club activities down on our college applications. Suddenly, being "extracurricular" mattered tremendously. How would college admissions of-

fices know that all my two years in the French club meant
was that I could bake *gâteau chocolat* as well as angel
food? So it wasn't all for nothing. Then there were the
boys, who wheeled past (they just happened to be in the
neighborhood) to see what was up and to eat free cookies,
and we laughed dumb-femininely at their smart comments,
pretended to be hurt when they said the cake frosting tasted like car grease, because after all, without them we
might have decorations, but we wouldn't have dates. Some
of us didn't anyway. For those there was compensation in
the leftovers—the broken cookies and the loaves of
French bread someone had returned for a refund because
the dough was unbaked in the middle. We often ate more
than we sold, nibbling through our wares as if God or
Providence made an exception for broken cookies and
crumbs of fudge. But on Monday morning we'd be dieting
again, of course, with celery sticks held like cigarettes between our fingers as we planned who'd bake what next
Saturday.

AFTER the launching of Friendship 7, the first U.S. orbital spaceship—we were in second grade, and, gathered around a TV in the gym, we joined in the countdown, out loud: ten, nine, eight, seven . . .—after that, NASA held little interest for most of us. I watched the first space walk, hoping, I think, for Major White's cord to snap and send him off in space (just as I hoped on "Dr. Kildare" for incurable disease) and imagining what it would be like to die floating in space. I watched the moon walk too, but after the first novelty and the realization that no moon men would appear, that there would be no oxygen leaks or short circuits, I turned off the set and haven't seen a space walk since.

There was so little drama to it all, everything charted and predictable, double checked, A-OK, over and out. What we wanted was the thrill of the unexpected. Sometimes we got it from real life episodes—an assassination, an election scandal, a mass murder—but never in the space program. It seemed that real life had been upstaged for us by scripted, manufactured dramas on the screen. Gemini and Apollo, "One small step for man . . . ," un-glamorous-looking astronauts' wives and short-haired, pale-faced astronauts (even their beards, at splashdown, seemed crew-cut), and the minor excitements created by a broken TV camera or a lunar module delay—none of them could compete with "Lost in Space" or "Star Trek's" Mr. Spock and his zippered, jump-suited crew, battling "The Blob" or space fever. Magazines filled their coverage of the space shots with what's called, I guess, the "human angle"—the tuna sandwich some astronaut ate once in the cabin, their "gees" and "gollys," their in-flight references to Snoopy and the World Series, and the knowledge that astronauts drink Tang too. All of that took from the strangeness of space, brought it closer to home, made walking on the moon seem to us like jogging around the block. NASA robbed us of mystery, diminished the appeal of a once-forbidden fruit by increasing its attainability. (Suddenly we could get pomegranates in the supermarket. Moon rocks next?) No wonder, now, we have a science-fiction passion, a love of the occult, no wonder that Flash Gordon has suddenly reappeared at campus film festivals, or that we read our horoscopes daily and talk of witches.

When we were seventeen, my friend Laura changed her name to Lucifera (Lucy for short) and announced she was a witch. She had always looked the part, a bit—very tall, very skinny, with strange, sharp features—and now, in her blue lipstick and long black gowns, with a locker she grew cobwebs and mushrooms in, until the principal ordered her to clean it out ("A hex on *him*," she said) she looked even more like one. Lucifera's witch transformation came on the cusp of the supernatural era, when *Rosemary's Baby* was born and astrology became fashionable, but it was more than just a fad, I think, taken on with obsessive energy—a game, at first, perhaps, that turned dead serious. Lucifera read old tracts on the subject, studied medieval documents, memorized chants and spells. Rumors spread—all true—that she slept in a graveyard and that the bloody marks on her arms and legs came from self-inflicted scratches made by her inch-long fingernails.

People laughed at her—her strangeness uniting us in a comfortable, shared normality—but she frightened us too.

There is a scrap of doubt in all of us, ready to latch onto things outside the realm of biology books; we all carry with us the memory of strange unexplained events and when we meet a girl like Lucifera, we tend to pool our doubts and memories, like Girl Scouts trading ghost stories around a camp fire. Full moons and dark nights, voodoo dolls and stinging herbs and howling witchcraft left us uneasy. I saw the dirt under Lucifera's purple fingernails and the Band-Aid box she kept her deadly nightshade in, but there were others who really *believed*, who saw only witchness, a few peripheral ninth-grade girls and an unloved outsider of a math-brain boy, and they attached themselves to Lucifera and to witchcraft, having a label, at last, for their outsiderness. As witches, they could flaunt it.

They trouble me, these groups that band together with only their differences from the rest in common—these alliances that misfits make. Their eighteen-hour marathons, locked up together in a tiny room, till one of them reaches hysteria, their talk of "evil," and the car accidents and illnesses that prove them right—their talk of evil turned out to be an evil in itself, and really dangerous. It spreads; strangeness and fear always do, as normality doesn't. As once we attributed the unexplainable to God, and trusted and accepted it, now we may attribute it to witchcraft and the occult, and tamper with it.

The witchcraft plague is surely a jackpot for television, and the new shows are full of it, because it's chilling and dramatic, of course, without requiring explanation and the usual end-of-program tying up of strings or, for that matter, having to make any pretense at good sense. One program last year, I remember, dealt with a 1970s murderer (a vampire, the authorities suspected) who left his corpses drained of blood. I kept watching the show, in spite of my feeling that this was not just a bad program but a very ugly one, an *evil* one, because I wanted to see what rational explanation they would cook up at the end (a medical student practicing transfusions? an escaped mental patient?), but discovered instead that the killer really *was* a vampire, 1972-style, coffin, fangs and all. And when he was apprehended, as of course he had to be, it was by vampire-catching means (using a Bible and a crucifix) which left me feeling that, because the L.A. police force put themselves out for *him,* he'd really won. I'm overly protective of the viewing audience, perhaps, but I think the distinction between fantasy and reality is blurry enough without vampires and straight, Dragnet-type cops sharing one bill. We're left uneasy, nervous, doubtful, and ready to pounce on victims like those Salem villagers more than two centuries ago.

Witches ... vampires ... with station breaks in between. Our 1960s upbringing has left us disbelieving and gullible at the same time, ready to accept everything or nothing.

Pollution and overpopulation have built up slowly, but our awareness of them came all at once, in 1969. Suddenly the word *ecology* was everywhere. We were juniors the year we all read Ehrlich's *Population Bomb* and felt again the kind of fear that hadn't really touched us since the air-raid drills of 1962. Not personal, individual fear but end-of-the-world fear, that by the time we were our parents' age we would be sardine-packed and tethered to our gas masks in a skyless cloud of smog. Partly because the idea of pollution hit us so suddenly, and from behind (just when we were alerted to the possibility of quite a different kind of shock, and expending our fury over the war), the realization that our resources were disappearing hit us hard. We were a generation unused to thinking ahead, incapable of visualizing even our twenties, and faced suddenly with the prospects of the year 2000 and forced, in youth, to contemplate the bleakness of our middle age.

We were raised to trust science and technology above all else, and now scientists and technologists were telling us that almost nothing could be done to save us. It seemed unfair that this should happen in our lifetimes when it was not our fault—that we should limit ourselves to just two children to make up for past generations that didn't. For the first time in my life, I remember wishing I'd been born in an earlier time and being thankful that at least I hadn't been born ten years later. All my sensibilities were heightened—sometimes I caught myself aware of my breathing (an act I'd never really thought about); I began to notice trash cans and litter baskets and pregnant women (there seemed so many of them. I was indignant—they were using up the quota, filling spaces that should have been left for the children of my friends and me).

Like one of Dr. Kildare's cancer patients, I felt condemned to death. Hope was held out, of course. There was Earth Day, celebrated at our school by the announcement that no one was to drive his car that day, and by a litter clean-up campaign that lasted for two hours while we attacked the beer cans on one half-mile stretch of highway. The president of our Environment Protection club (every new cause becomes a club sooner or later, and ends up holding dances) announced that we could help by cutting down on electric power, giving up our hairdryers and radios for the sake of A Better Tomorrow and boycotting the soft drinks in the nonrecycleable containers. Halfheartedly I went through the motions, but my sacrifices seemed too far removed, too small a drop in the bucket. The fact that, if everybody did it, our resources would be saved ("*Some*body has to be first . . ." said our club president) meant little when, looking over your shoulder, you'd notice no one following. The connection between cause and effect was impossible to see and so, like the taking of vitamins (another never-wholly-real or trusted activity I went through without apparent benefit) my litter picking and boycotting grew less and less fervent. The old hopeless urgency expired; we'd almost grown accustomed to our death sentences.

We feel cheated, many of us—the crop of 1953—which is why we complain about inheriting problems we didn't cause. (Childhood notions of justice, reinforced by Perry Mason, linger on. Why should I clean up someone else's mess? Who can I blame?) We're excited also, of course: I can't wait to see how things turn out. But I wish I weren't quite so involved, I wish it weren't my life that's being turned into a suspense thriller.

AT seventeen, in my senior year, I left Oyster River High and entered Phillips Exeter Academy. Something strange got into the boys that year, as if, along with the legendary salt peter, something like lust for the country was being sprinkled into the nightly mashed potatoes. It wasn't just the overalls (with a tie on top to meet the dress code) or the country music that came humming out of every dorm. Exonians—Jonathan Juniors and Carter the Thirds, Latin scholars and mathematicians with 800s on their college boards—were suddenly announcing to the college placement counselor that no, they didn't want a Harvard interview, not now or ever. Hampshire, maybe (that's the place where you can go and study Eastern Religion or dulcimer-making). But many weren't applying anyplace—they were going to study weaving in Norway, to be shepherds in the Alps, deckhands on a fishing boat or—most often—farmers. After the first ecological fury died down, after Ehrlich's *Population Bomb* exploded, that's what we were left with. Prep school boys felt it more than most, perhaps, because they, more than most, had worked their minds at the expense of their hands.

And now, their heads full of theorems and declensions, they wanted to get back to the basics—to the simple, honest, uncluttered life where manure was cow shit, not bovine waste.

Exeter's return to the soil took the form of the farm project; a group of boys who got together sold a few stocks, bought a red pick-up truck and proposed, for a spring project, that they work a plot of school-owned land a few miles out of town. The country kids I went to Oyster River with, grown up now and working in the shoe factory or married—they would have been amused at the farming fairy tale. In March, before the ice thawed, the harvest was already being planned. The faculty protested and the project died, and most—not all—went on to college in the fall. (They talk now, from a safe distance, about the irrelevances of Spenser and the smell of country soil and fresh-cut hay.) A friend who really did go on to farming came to visit me at college the next fall. He looked out of place in the dorm; he put his boots up on my desk and then remembered he had cow dung on the soles. He laughed when I reminded him about the farm project. It's best they never tried, I think. That way, in ten years, when they're brokers, they'll still have the dream: tomatoes big as pumpkins, pumpkins big as suns and corn that's never known the touch of blight.

When I was eighteen, a friend who was a debutante that year invited me to the Junior League's annual coming-out ball. I almost didn't go—I didn't have a dress or shoes; I worried about whether to wear gloves or not, and how to avoid wearing my yellow vinyl jacket if it rained. I borrowed a dress, finally, bought shoes, pinned up my hair and, since it didn't rain, went coatless, hoping the hole in my gloves and the grape juice stain on my skirt wouldn't show, marking me instantly, among the debutantes and Honored Guests, for what I was—a slightly second-hand outsider.

I needn't have worried about that. I may have stood out, but if I did, it was because I'd overdressed. The ones who really belonged wore their hair down, kicked off their shoes, compared one another's rummage-sale bow ties and baggy dinner jackets. The debutantes, many of them, made loud and laughing explanations why they'd come out at all ("Isn't it the silliest thing you've ever heard?!!!") and tried as nearly as they could to disassociate themselves from everything that had made them Junior Leaguers in the first place. Money and social position—earned with such unquestioning struggle by our parents' generation—is for us (now that we have it, if we do) something of an embarrassment. *We* have not gone through the Depression or walked ten miles to school or eaten bacon fat for supper. Whether or not we're rich—and I'm speaking not just for the few who are—not many of us grew up really poor. (Deprivation was a fifty-cent allowance and a black and white TV.) So we don't have the respect for money that our parents had. In fact, it's more a source of guilt. We use it, of course, for our European summers, our college educations, our hairdryers and electric typewriters and ten-speed bicycles, but we romanticize the lives of those without it—people who we, the young, affluent and educated, see with a new sentimentality for The Great Midwest, as the Real Americans inhabiting The Real World. The self-employed farmer, the truck-stop waitress, the lobster fisherman—they are perhaps the closest thing my generation has to heroes.

We play at poverty, proudly broadcasting the occasional destitution brought on by the unexpected expense of a new needle for the stereo or tires for the car; we speak—in front of blacks particularly—of how we never could have gone to college without such a good scholarship. Summers we go slumming as waitresses and construction workers; back at school we reminisce about our happy days as "menials" ("It's such a great feeling, working with your hands . . ."), the fondness coming from the knowledge we won't be spending our whole lives waiting on tables, living off tips and leftover soup *du jour*. I cannot really criticize—I do it too—but I can comment. It would be silly to wish we didn't have the comfort we have. I could wish, though, that, having it, we didn't pretend otherwise. Admiring poverty or simplicity for its own sake, with guilt and condescension, seems misguided. What we're really doing is acting poor and living rich, scorning money while living as tidily subsidized students, getting paid simply to read and think.

Our snobbery has reversed itself now so that, while ghetto inhabitants still strive for Cadillacs, the rest—the ones who have the luxury not to care—are buying '57 Chevys. Shabby overalls that show the mark of having worked the fields and ankle-length cotton dusters, faded from a hundred washings, and denim work shirts with the elbows worn right through are more than fashion fads, they're evidences of this playing-poor routine. Some of us cultivate it in our speech—twanging a little, saying our -ing words southern style, like huntin', readin', farmin' and, a favorite verb, "truckin'." To us—the summer-vacation home-folk, the weekend farmers, the rummage sale customers who pay by check—a gas-pump job seems almost romantic and hitchhiking is the preferred means of travel, not because it's cheaper but because it's how you meet "the *real* people."

Just about every suburban-born, college-bred boy I know has a hitchhiking story about "this real great truck driver" he met, the kind of salt-of-the-earth, natural man who hasn't read a book in twenty years but who, his hitch-hiking passengers tell me, "knows what it's all about." He's usually called Joe or Red, this potato-and-beef hauling everyman, and his life's a little tragic (he sleeps in the cab of his truck and spends Christmas on the road, staring out at colored lights blinking through windows), but it is simple, honest, free. He is a philosopher of the road who has given the boy—because *this* boy is *special*—some parting nugget of Truth as he lets him out at Exit 1 for New Haven or Exit 23 for Cambridge, some words of wisdom the boy now imparts to me, over coffee and deeply inhaled nonfilter cigarettes in the campus grill.

We're all in search of sages. Information surrounds us. Facts about North Vietnamese dead and grams of carbohydrate in Rice Krispies and points lost on the stock exchange and TV stars' divorces are drilled into us like lists of vocabulary words for college boards. Oh, the new trend in education, while we were in school, leaned toward "concepts" and away from what we called "specifics." Vagueness—we called it bullshitting—was often easy on our high school essay question exams. But in spite of the generalities we met with at school, there was a feeling of being overwhelmed by details. Every succeeding gener-

ation has just that many more years of history to study—
more presidents, more planets (Pluto had not yet been discovered when my father was in school. Neither had
DNA). We were bombarded outside the classroom most
of all by—it's a cliché, but it's true too—the constantly
expanding forces of the media, magazines too numerous to
fit in the racks, TVs in every house and even, later, in a
lot of dormitory rooms and car radios we're so accustomed to that only when they're turned off do we notice
they were on. A whole new area of expertise has been developed (it should be a college major, and will be someday soon, perhaps): the field of trivia. TV game shows,
awarding cars and minks and refrigerator-freezers to the
ones who know the most cereal-box-type information,
have glorified it for us. Watching those shows I am
amazed to discover how much I know, without knowing I
knew it. I answer bonus questions without thinking, like
the reincarnated Bridey Murphy speaking in a dialect she
claimed she'd never heard.

All of which cannot help cluttering the mind. It's an un-
scientific notion that, like a cupboard, the brain has only
so many shelves, before things start to crowd and fall out,
but I often get the feeling that I haven't space left to
spread out my thoughts and see what I have. Loose links
clanking in my head, and no chain, I long for—capital
W—Wisdom. We all do, I think, in this era of overly
data-processed, glutted computers. Teachers were rarely
funds of knowledge for us (they seldom knew more than
what the textbooks taught, keeping one step ahead, reading the chapters a day before they were assigned).
Parents, cautioned in the age of permissiveness not to over-
burden with advice, and confused, themselves, sometimes
to the point of despair, could give little. The venerable
God died during our youth. (I still remember the orange
and black cover of *Time* magazine one week—"Is God
Dead?"—the phrase and the notion were brand-new then,
and though he'd never been alive for me in the first place,
the idea of his death, death of one of the few existing
sages—even a mythical one—disturbed me.)

Indeed, so many of our childhood authority figures
made a point of *not* being profound, wary of being
laughed at for seriousness by what they took to be a

sharp, tough, unsentimental bunch of smart-aleck cynics. Actually, we didn't turn out that way at all. My contemporaries surprise me for what is at times their mushiness—their damp-eyed reading of *Love Story* and the thin volumes of Rod McKuen's emaciated poetry; their trust in the occult and all things astrological, following the daily horoscope with a faith they never gave, when we were younger and regarded as more gullible, to fortune-cookie prophecies and tea-leaf aphorisms.

The absence of true sages—men of deep sensibility, even, in our lives—leads us to make false gods of rock poets and grade-B philosophers, injecting comics and children's books with significance their authors never knew they had. We, who so hated school, are in search now of *teachers*. An apricot-robed, lotus-folded guru with a name too long to pronounce, an old man on a park bench, with a beard if possible, a plain-talking, no-nonsense Maine farmer with a pitchfork in his hand, the author of any slim volume of austere prose or poetry (the fewer words he writes, the more profound each one must be)—we attend their words so abjectly, sometimes even literally sit at their feet, waiting for any crumb of what will pass as wisdom to be offered us.

I remember a show-and-tell day when I was in fourth grade. I brought in a pot holder I'd woven, someone displayed a sea anemone and someone else explained the engine of his model car, and one boy brought his rosary beads and his crucifix, and took from his wallet a photograph of his priest and himself beside their church. We were all too stunned to laugh at first, but then the giggling started, until we were all hiccuping and one boy had to run off to the bathroom without waiting for a pass, and even the teacher was smiling, because religion was something shameful, the soft underside some of us had, but kept concealed, certainly. (Going to church was OK, like going to Brownies. But to speak, as Ralphie Leveque did, of loving God and of the blood of Christ, and Mary's tears and thorns and nails—that seemed almost dirty.)

Now, while the fourth graders might still giggle, Jesus has come out of the closet. The disenchanted, and the ones never enchanted in the first place, are returning to the fold with a passion their once-a-week religious parents never possessed. It is a sign of many things: an attempt to purify the spirit, to be drenched in holy waters after a drug-filled adolescence, a form of the new nostalgia, even—almost *camp*. What's really going on, though, in the Jesus movement, is our search for a prophet, for someone who can, for a change, tell us the answers. (The big line, in our school days, was "There is no right answer. What's your *opinion?*") After so many unprofound facts and so much loose, undisciplined freedom, it's comforting to have a creed to follow and a cross to bear.

Take a look at the windows of any up-to-date department store and you'll discover plenty about the mood of the country. For a while it was China—not just summit meetings with Chou En-lai, but stuffed pandas and (Mrs. Mao Tse-tung would be amused) newly stylish workers' pajamas just like the ones they wear in China. Pregnancy-simulating pillows (worn under smocks) were surely some kind of reaction to ZPG and abortion. First midiskirts, then hotpants told us something about the ups and downs of mood and daring; and now, well, now it's children's clothes.

Not for children. They are busy transcending childhood with toddler-sized bikinis and bell bottoms. But grown-ups and almost-grown-ups are turning, in this over-sophisticated world, to the reassuring simplicity of childhood. As I write this, the store windows are filled with pinafores and puffed sleeves, smocks and knee socks and Mary Janes and ponytails tied with ribbons or held in place with a plastic rabbit. Colors are pale pink and sky-blue and Easter-chick yellow; prints show Mickey Mouse and lollipops. Kids are in.

The trend goes beyond fashion. On college campuses there's a sudden interest in children—not in the detached, analytical perspective of child psychology, but in a way that attempts to recapture childhood for its students. (One of Yale's most popular seminars during my freshman year was a study of children's literature.) Students are far less likely to carry Piaget or Bruner than Andersen's *Fairy Tales, Winnie the Pooh, The Little Prince.* They write dissertations on comic books and tune in daily to "Mr. Rogers' Neighborhood" and "Sesame Street" (particularly good when stoned). It isn't just camp either; camp is for the cool steel-and-plastic territory of Andy Warhol and Ultra Violet. No tongue-in-cheek, no put-ons, no kidding: childhood and children are serious subjects.

Because they are closer than adults to instinct and because they suposedly haven't yet discovered the art of deception, children are viewed by my contemporaries, childhood-worshipers on the verge of adulthood, as the bearers of some ultimate wisdom. Children's books are examined for non-existent symbolism and their actions are imitated—in clothes and speech and movements and games —as if, by artificially reconstructing childhood, we could restore the innocence that goes along with it. It's a post-drug, post-free love reaction, maybe, the child vogue—an attempted return to the good old days when rules were laid down and life was simpler.

M Y GENERATION—the one that places so much
importance on *communication*—seems to be abandoning
language. Where once a person stopped to breathe or to
think, now he fills the gaps with passwords from a kind of
code that summons, in an instant, all that's young and hip
and *together*—rock music, patched blue jeans, bare feet,
Herman Hesse, marijuana and yoghurt. We no longer
need to say who we are; we can talk in a shorthand that
says everything for us. That's what "you know" really
means: *you know* what I mean, so why should I bother to
say it?

The new language is called colorful and expressive. Often it's pretty flat and repetitive, the same toneless superlatives and fuzzy adjectives repeated time and again until
"Far out" means nothing, because nothing is described as
less. The words are few—not enough to fill a dictionary
page but enough to build a vocabulary around: trip,
hassle, dig, head, man, together, where I'm at, like (half-
built bridge to a never-completed simile) and, of course,
you know. We no longer strive for eloquence. (Debating—the sport of the aristocracy—has been replaced

by rapping. Debaters remind us now of businessmen—
three-piece suits, brief cases filled with facts, no room for
feelings—whose rhetoric becomes the tool of evasiveness.)
Polished speech has come to be regarded almost as a form
of snobbery; adjectives, like color TV sets and second
cars, seem almost decadent. I find myself cultivating im-
purities in my speech, diluting thoughts with *ums* that
weren't there to begin with, mumbling, almost, and slow-
ing down to the new, 33⅓ rpm as if the thoughts that
come out are so complex they required all those pauses
for meditation. Few of them do.

Part of this comes from our return to nature, of course.
Language is an artifice and sometimes even a mask for
true feelings (do monkeys speak?...) while nonverbal
communication, the new catchword, is moving in to take
its place. (I was in junior high when the nonverbal business first struck. Suddenly book reports were to be sung or
danced or drawn or acted; make a collage, a diorama—
anything but a paragraph.) Emphasis has moved from *the
word* to *the spectacle,* and even Shakespeare, surely the
king of words, has been affected. I think of a performance
of *Measure for Measure* I acted in at college, with the
Duke making his fifth act entrance by swinging onstage
from a rope tied to a tree. The manner of his entrance
had no relation to the meaning of his lines, of course; the
impact was purely visual. The audience never really heard
the speech, in fact, because halfway down, the actor's rope
got stuck on a tree branch and left him hanging in mid-
air.

Drugs have something to do with the new language and
the new lethargy it exemplifies. Individual voices have become less and less identifiable in the great leveling-off process that attaches "wise" and "ize" to the ends of nouns
(moneywise ...), "hopefully" to the beginnings of sentences, and computer talk ("input, feedback") and clichés
like "generation gap" or "peer group" throughout. Communication, too, has become a cliché, but the problem of
communicating is now a very real one. As the quality of
our language degenerates, so does the quality of communication—and the quality of thought.

Sometimes I conceal the fact that I've never smoked a joint. Occasionally I lie, regretting it later, ashamed that I should be ashamed. Now smoking (grass) has become a second form of virginity, rarer even than the first. There are some people now who've been through it all and given up on grass, but their abstinence is different from mine, worldier. I catch myself, sometimes, unwilling to admit that I don't smoke because we judge by surfaces these days (I do too) and if a person's liberated and hip and creative-thinking ("liberal-minded" is a dead term now; LBJ was "liberal" to us once), then he smokes, and if he's dull and crew-cut and Republican, if he listens to the Fifth Dimension and Mantovani, then he doesn't. More important is the corollary, though, by which anyone who smokes is liberated, hip etc. (season ticket to the arts, pass key to Deep Thoughts without philosophy courses), and anyone who doesn't smoke is, if not crew-cut and Republican, old-fashioned, certainly, and cowardly, probably a tight-lipped churchgoer (though not religious in the *cosmic* sense of those whose minds are dope-freed, hip to Jesus).

Oh, it's not quite that simple. As smoking dope has become common (grass, hash and pills more easily accessible), membership in the club has come to demand more. Seventh graders, high school cheerleaders, New York executives all smoke, and though we love the sense of a huge fellowship (bred, as we were, from the committee book report on up, to expect and enjoy participation in some kind of group), membership loses value if all exclusiveness is lost. The strongest group alliances are worked for (that Woodstock glow—people who've been there say outsiders could never understand—where rain and mud provided for survival of the fittest, so those who stayed through shared something in common, and though they were three hundred thousand, they were one kind of members-only club). It's no longer distinctive and original enough simply to smoke; entrance to the Elite requires more—which only means that *not* smoking separates you even further than it used to. The ones who, like me, don't smoke, may not be seen as square exactly, but a distance is established. A smoker and a nonsmoker are seldom really close. Often I'm spoken to almost as a foreigner—not loud, and slowly, so I'll understand, but formally, as if I were years

younger or deprived of my sense of touch or taste or smell
and ignorant, therefore, of a whole realm, as if I were a
teacher or a parent or a college admissions officer.

All this might seem reason enough to smoke. I certainly
don't worry that I'd become addicted, that my mind would
blur and my hands begin to shake or, as we used to be
warned, that marijuana "leads to the hard stuff." Marijuana smoking isn't important enough to rate deliberations
(like spending half an hour—will I or won't I?—agonizing
over whether to eat ice cream or not, and then what flavor, jimmies or not, and sugar cone or waffle). But the
fact that, for some people (a good many of the ones who
use drugs, and that's what it seems like to me, very often—*using*) they have taken on this disproportionate importance, that's what keeps me unindulgent when the
people in the room I'm in (often friends) turn on. When
everyone around you is high, it's not a pleasant feeling,
being—what is the word?—low? And why should what is
natural and normal suddenly be *low?* What bothers me
most is that it matters so much whether you do or not. I
once explained my feelings to a boy at school—"Why do
people ask whether I smoke, and never whether I listen to
Beethoven or what I read or whether I can make a chocolate mousse?"—and at the end of my long, debater-like
pronouncement he nodded and said, "Yeah, you're right.
But you still haven't told me: do you smoke or not?"

On top of that, many little prejudices. I don't like what
I think of as drug language—those *likes* and *you knows*
that fill the spaces where people used to breathe and think,
and the same lack of precision that affects writing sometimes, when accompanying photographs make description
unnecessary, only here the fuzziness comes from the
knowledge that we've all been there and know what it's
like and no comment is necessary. Drugs have become—
like hair length and record collection—a symbol for who
you are, and you can't be all those other things: Progres-
sive and Creative and Free Thinking—without taking that
crumpled role of dry brown vegetation and holding it to
your lips. You are what you eat—or what you smoke, or
what you don't smoke. And when you say "like, you
know" you're speaking the code, and suddenly the music
of the Grateful Dead and the poetry of Bob Dylan and

the general brilliance of Ken Kesey all belong to you as if, in those three fuzzy, mumbled words, you'd created art yourself and uttered the wisdom of the universe.

One other thing. Almost surely this will sound stuffy and righteous, and once again I feel defensiveness approaching (no, I really am not in the crew-cut league, and I guess I betray my own superficiality of judgment in even caring that I'll be accused of that). But, all that said, I don't believe in unearned gifts. The psychological releases that supposedly come from the use of dope—the heightened perceptions, new sounds ("You haven't really heard Beethoven until you've listened to him stoned"), the "far-out" colors—they all seem too easily come by to be deserved, to be *true*. It's unacceptable to me that mental and spiritual "enlightenment" may be bought for the price of an ounce of marijuana, and that a simple physical act like lighting up a joint and inhaling (no skill required there) should equip one to listen to the Ninth Symphony with a richness and amplitude that Beethoven himself never enjoyed.

It's always seemed odd to me that although not everyone pretends to be interested in art, or drama, or literature or dance, nearly everyone my age claims to be "into" music, meaning, usually, not that they play but that they listen or, more precisely, that they turn on the stereo and take out the night's chemistry assignment, or that they spend hours flipping through albums at a record store or studying hi-fi magazines, constantly building onto their already enormous system of amplifiers, headphones, turntables and tuners so that the mechanics of music-loving almost drowns out the music. The fact that it is a mostly-male obsession, of course, seems suspicious too (do women actually care less about music?), all of which leads me to believe that genuinely caring about music has very little to do with buying records and speakers.

What we are interested in is music, all right—art, culture, sensitivity—but not all of us have it; some people are simply born with tin ears, some people would be well advised to stick to medicine or math, not poetry. Being sensitive and "artsy" is important just now though, and, while it's impossible to fake it with a violin or a piano, anyone

who has the money can buy a stereo and *listen*—a passive
poet soul. Suddenly the arts and everything they represent—passion and romance, and, in an odd way, sex (if
a boy can't turn on a girl, maybe Mozart or the Stones
can)—suddenly all that is as purchasable as a car. As
once, I suppose, some people decorated their walls with
the suitable books, in all the right bindings, now we buy
listening apparatus. Not that we don't really listen, and
like to listen, and not that the music isn't, sometimes, really worth listening to. Music has become a status-building
device, though. I feel it in myself—pride at my own wall
of albums and curiosity about the musical tastes of ac-
quaintances. And if their wall matches mine, I think more
of them, and if their collection is inferior, or their record
player weak, I must fight the impulse to reject their sensi-
tivities. That's wrong, I know. Not loving music doesn't
make one boorish, first of all, and not playing records
doesn't mean one doesn't love music. We, with our overin-
dulged senses, forget that sometimes; we feel the need for
constant sensory stimulation, a bombardment, from all
sides, of sounds and tastes and colors, which amounts not
to the heightened perceptivity we boast of, but finally to
numbness, anaesthesia.

FOR ABOUT three weeks of my freshman year at college I had two roommates instead of one—the girl in the bottom bunk and her friend, who made our quarters especially cramped because, in addition to being six feet tall with lots of luggage, he was male. We slept in shifts—they together, until I came back to the room at night, then he outside in the living room on the couch, until she got up, then he in her bed and I in mine, or I in hers and he in mine, because it was easier for me to get out from the bottom without waking him, and he needed his sleep.... We never made it a threesome, but the awkwardness was always there (those squeaking bedsprings ...), as it was for many girls I knew, and many boys. Coming back to the room and announcing my presence loudly with a well-directed, well-projected cough or a casual murmur, "Hmmm—I think I'll go to my room now," it occurred to me that it wasn't my roommate but I—the one who slept alone, the one whose only pills were vitamins and aspirin—I was the embarrassed one. How has it happened, what have we come to, that the scarlet letter these days isn't A, but V?

137

In the beginning, of course, everyone's a virgin. You start on equal footing with everyone else (sex is something comic and dirty—the subject of jokes and slumber-party gossip), but pretty soon the divisions form. (Sex is still dirty, but less unthinkable, sort of thrilling.) There's the girl with the older boy friend (he's in ninth grade); the girl who went away to summer camp and fell in love! the girl who kisses boys right out there on the dance floor for all the junior high to see. (That's the point, of course. If she wanted it to be a secret, she'd have gone out to the Coke machine with him, the way the other couples do.) But everybody's still a virgin. The question isn't even asked.

The first to go is usually a secretarial student, the one who started wearing bras in fourth grade, the one who pierced her ears in sixth, the one who wears purple eyeshadow to school. She doesn't talk about it, but she doesn't make a big thing of keeping it quiet either, so word gets around, and all the *good* girls whisper about her—they knew it all the time, what can you expect? She's probably older anyway, she must have stayed back a couple of years....

Then, maybe in tenth grade, or eleventh, (if you live in a city, make that ninth), it's a good girl, one of your crowd. (You know because she called her best friend up the next day and—promise not to tell—told her.) At first you think it was a mistake: he took advantage of her, she didn't know what was happening—and you feel terribly, terribly sorry for her and wonder how she'll ever face him again. But she does; in fact, she's with him all the time now—*doing it again* most likely. You stare at her in the halls ("she doesn't *look* any different") and, though she's still your friend—you still pass notes in math class— there's a distance between you now. Woman of the world and little girl—hot ticket and (for the first time, the word sounds slightly unpleasant) *virgin.*

After that, the pattern becomes more common. The girl, when she breaks up with that first boy, can hardly hold out on his successor. And her ex-boy friend's new girl friend, naturally, has an expectation to satisfy if she wants a date to the prom. More and more girls are, in the words of those who aren't, *going all the way.* As for the ones

who still baby-sit on Friday nights, or the ones whose
dates are still getting up the courage to kiss them good
night, they spend their time speculating—"does she or
doesn't she?" (It's always the *girl* who does; not a combined act at all so much as an individual one.) The group
of shocked guessers gets smaller and smaller until they—
you, if you're still one of them—realize that the ones to be
whispered about, stared at, shocked by, aren't the others
now but themselves. It's hard to say at what point the moment occurs, but suddenly virginity isn't fun anymore. The
days when it was taken for granted are long gone; so are
the days when it was half and half (The Virgins vs. the
Nons). The ones who *aren't* now take that for granted,
and as for the ones who are, well—they don't talk about it
much. Virginity has become not a flower or a jewel, a pre-
cious treasure for Prince Charming or a lively, prized and
guarded gift, but a dusty relic—an anachronism. Most of
all, it's an embarrassment.

So here we have this baffled, frightened virgin (she's third
person now; I can't help wanting to disassociate myself
from her category and all it seems to represent). She may
not really be a prude or an iceberg (maybe nobody's ever
tried . . .) but that's how the world views her. She's on the
same team with Sensible Orthopedic Shoes and Billy Gra-
ham and Lawrence Welk and the Republican party. Old
ladies—her grandmother's friends—love her (she can get
a date with their favorite nephews any time) and wonder
sadly why there aren't more girls around like that. A certain kind of man (boy) is very fond of her, too. He's the
timid type—just as glad, really, not to feel that he's expected to perform. (He's an embarrassed virgin too, and
the last thing these two need is each other, perpetuating
the breed—as their nonvirginal contemporaries, in love-
making, perpetuate the race—by nonperformance.) The
sexual revolution is on, but the virgin isn't part of it.

The sexual revolution. It's a cliché, but it exists all
right, and its pressures are everywhere. All the old excuses
("I might get pregnant," "I'm not that kind of girl") are
gone. Safe and increasingly available contraceptives (for
anyone brave and premeditative enough to get them)
make pre-marital sex possible; changing moral standards,

an increased naturalness, make it commonplace; elegant
models of sexual freedom—Julie Christie, Catherine
Deneuve—have made it fashionable. Consider a virgin in
the movies. Is there a single pretty young heroine who
doesn't hop unself-consciously into bed? (Who is there left
for her to identify with—Doris Day?) Then there are
magazines, filled with discussions of intricate sexual problems (the timing of orgasms ... do I get one? do I give
one?) while the virgin remains on a whole other level—
her fears compounded. (Our old, junior high notion of sex
was that it got done to you; the girl with the purple eyeshadow just let it happen. Today all kinds of problems in
technique make the issue much more complicated for an
inexperienced media-blitzed girl: not just *will I* but *can
I*.) The people who've been making nice, simple love for
years now, while the virgin became more and more
unique, have, quite understandably, gone on to other
things. There is foreplay and afterplay and the 999 positions of the *Kamasutra*. . . . The train has left the station
before the virgin's bought her ticket or even, maybe,
packed her bags.

There are other pressures too, less remote than the
images on a screen or the words on a page. Though individuality is officially admired, "Peer-group pressure" (a
fifties concept) is very real when it comes to sex. Other
girls assume a friend's sexual experience. So, more impor-
tantly, do the men she goes out with. The death of the
formal date (with dinner and the theater, high heels and a
good-night kiss afterward) has put a new ambiguity on
male-female relationships. Just sitting around, talking and
listening to music, while it may be lots more real and honest and all those other good 1973-type adjectives, is also
lots more difficult for a virgin to cope with. If this is
someone she likes—but doesn't love—there isn't any way
for her to demonstrate simple fondness. The kiss that once
said "I like you" now seems a promise of something more
to come. And if, perhaps, she's decided that yes, this is
someone she would sleep with, she may discover (final
irony) that he isn't eager, when he finds out she's a virgin,
to be the first. The situation seems unresolvable: virginity
is a self-perpetuating condition. (Like the unskilled, unem-
ployed worker, the virgin hears—time and again—"Come

back when you've got some experience.") The only way out seems to be the crudest, most loveless and mechanical way possible: almost a reverse prostitution. It happens— as once young boys would be initiated in a brothel—because the idea now, for the late-bloomer, the high school baby-sitter—the idea is to get it over with as quickly, painlessly and forgettably as possible.

If it hasn't happened before, the pressure is really on at college. I'm looking back now to the beginning of my freshman year. What I should remember is my first glimpse of the college campus, freshman assembly, buying notepads and textbooks and writing my name and my dorm on the covers. Instead, my memory of September blurs into a single word: sex. Not that Yale was the scene of one continuous orgy. But we surely were preoccupied. Ask a friend how things were going and he'd tell you whether or not he'd found a girl. Go to a freshman women's tea or a Women's Liberation meeting and talk would turn, inevitably, to contraceptives and abortions. Liberated from the restrictions imposed by parents and curfews and car seats (those tiny Volkswagens), we found ourselves suddenly sharing a world not with the junior high and the ninth grade, but with college seniors and graduate students— men and women in their twenties. Very quickly, we took on their values, imitated their behavior and, often, swallowed their pills.

September was a kind of catching-up period for all the people who hadn't cut loose before. All that first week, girls trooped up the stairs at 3 and 4 A.M., and sometimes not at all. Fall, for the freshmen, at least, was a frantic rush of pairing off, with boys running for the girls and, strangely enough (there were so few of us, so many boys to go around) the girls rushing for the boys and the couples, finally, rushing for the beds as if this were musical chairs and if you didn't hurry you'd be left standing up. It was maybe the last chance to be clumsy and amateurish and virginal. After that, you entered the professional league where, if you weren't a pro, you had a problem.

I don't mean to reinforce the embarrassment, to confirm the hopelessness of the virgin's situation—"yes, things are pretty bad, aren't they?"—or to frighten anyone about to embark upon the brave new world of college or job-

and-apartment. Because as a matter of fact there shouldn't be anything scary or hopeless or embarrassing about virginity any more than there should be anything scary, hopeless or embarrassing about the loss of it. I'm not *for* virginity or *against* pre-marital sex, and I'm certainly not defending virginity for its own sake—the I'm-saving-it-for-my-husband line. Whether or not you're a virgin isn't the point; the question is what *kind* of a virgin or a non-virgin you are, and whether you are what you are by choice or by submission to outside pressures. (Plenty of "freely consenting" adults are really victims of a cultural, everybody's-doing-it type of forced consent.) Some women can easily and naturally love a man or want to be close to him, maybe even without love. I have a friend like that—a girl I used to think of as promiscuous and hypocritical when she said of each new boy friend (and sometimes two at once), "I love him." I see now this was quite genuine. She has a giving and sharing nature and she loves very easily. She isn't racking up points in her sexual relationships; she truly wants to know as many people as she can. Not everyone can be that way; knowing someone means being known, giving up privacy in a manner that's difficult for many people. These days one's privacy is no longer one's own. Even the act of refusing to give it up is intruded upon. It's no longer just the nonvirgin who subjects herself to intense scrutiny; now it's the virgin whose very refusal is scrutinized, maybe even more closely than her surrender would be. People don't talk much about who's on the pill or who's sleeping together, but there's endless speculation about who isn't. "What's the matter with her?" they ask. Is she frigid? Lesbian? Big-brother types offer helpful advice, reasoning that if she isn't interested in them except as a friend, something must indeed be wrong with her. Her abstinence, in short, is fair game for everyone.

Privacy—and freedom—can be maintained only by disregarding the outside pressures. Freedom is choosing, and sometimes that may mean choosing not to be "free." For the embarrassed virgin, unsure now whether her mind is her own ("Do I really want to go to bed with him, or do I simply want to be like everybody else?")—for her, there's a built-in test. If she really wants to, on her own, she won't have to ask herself or be embarrassed. Her inexperience and clumsiness will have, for him, a kind of coltish grace. Our grandparents, after all, never read the *Kamasutra,* and here we are today, proof that they managed fine without it.

1972

Everyone is raised on nursery rhymes and nonsense stories. But it used to be that when you grew up the nonsense disappeared. Not for us—it is at the core of our music and literature and art and, in fact, of our lives. Like characters in an Ionesco play, we take absurdity unblinking. In a world where military officials tell us "We had to destroy the village in order to save it," Dylan lyrics make an odd kind of sense. They aren't meant to be understood; they don't jar our sensibilities because we're used to non sequiturs. We don't take anything too seriously these days. (Was it a thousand earthquake victims or a million? Does it matter?) The casual butcher's operation in the film *M*A*S*H* and the comedy in Vonnegut and the album cover showing John and Yoko, backs bare are all part of the new absurdity. The days of the Little Moron joke and the elephant joke and the knock-knock joke are gone. It sounds melodramatic, but the joke these days is life.

You're not supposed to care too much any more. Reactions have been scaled down from screaming and jelly-bean-throwing to nodding your head and maybe—if the music really gets to you (and music's the only thing that does any more)—tapping a finger. We need a passion transfusion, a shot of energy in the veins. It's what I'm most impatient with, in my generation—this languid, I-don't-give-a-shit-ism that stems in part, at least, from a culture of put-ons in which any serious expression of emotion may be branded sentimental and old-fashioned. The fact that we set such a premium on being cool reveals a lot about us: the idea is not to care. You can hear it in the speech of college students today: cultivated monotones, low volume, punctuated with four-letter words that come off sounding only bland. I feel it most of all on Saturday mornings, when the sun is shining and the crocuses about to bloom and, walking through the corridors of my dorm, I see there isn't anyone awake.

T O ME as a ten-year-old sixth grader in 1964, the Goldwater-Johnson election year was a drama, a six-month basketball playoff game, more action-packed than movies or TV. For all the wrong reasons, I loved politics and plunged into the campaign fight. Shivering in the October winds, outside a supermarket ("Hello, would you like some LBJ matches?"), Youth for Johnson tried hard to believe in the man with the ten-gallon hat. We were eager for a hero (we'd lost ours just ten months before) and willing to trust. Government deceit was not yet taken for granted—maybe because we were more naïve but also because the country was. Later, the war that never ended and the CIA and the Pentagon Papers and ITT would shake us, but in those days, when a man said "My fellow Americans . . ." we listened.

At school I was a flaming liberal, holding lunchroom debates and setting up a ten-year-old's dichotomies: if you were for Johnson, you were "for" the Negroes (we called them Negroes then, not *blacks*) if you were for Goldwater you were against them. Equally earnest Republicans would expound the domino theory and I would waver in spite of myself (what they said sounded logical) knowing there was a fallacy somewhere but saying only "If my father was here, he'd explain it . . ."

A friend and I set up a campaign headquarters at school under a huge ALL THE WAY WITH LBJ sign. (The tough kids snickered at that—"all the way" was reserved for the behavior of fast girls in the janitor's closet at dances.) The pleasures we got from our LBJ headquarters and its neat stacks of buttons and pamphlets was much the same as the pleasure I got, five years later, manning the "Support your Junior Prom" bake sale table in the lobby at school. I liked playing store, no matter what the goods.

And I believed, then, in the power of dissent and the possibility for change. I wrote protest songs filled with bloody babies and starving Negroes, to the tune of "America the Beautiful." I marched through the streets of town, a tall candle flickering in my hand, surrounded by college kids with love beads and placards (what they said seems mild and polite now). I remember it was all "so beautiful" I cried, but when I try to recapture the feeling, nothing comes. Like a sharp pain or the taste of peach ice cream on a hot July day, the sensation lasts only as long as the stimulus.

Gene McCarthy must have encountered blizzards in 1968, and mill towns like Berlin, N.H.—where I went to campaign for George McGovern—must have smelled just as bad as they do now. But back then those things made the fight even more rewarding, because in suffering for your candidate and your dreams you were demonstrating love. But in 1972, there was nothing fun about air so smelly you bought perfume to hold under your nose or snow falling so thick you couldn't make out the words on the Yorty billboard right in front of you. No one felt moved to build snowmen.

Campaigning in New Hampshire was work. Magazines and newspapers blamed the absence of youth excitement on McGovern and said he lacked charisma—he wasn't a poet and his bumper stickers weren't daisy-shaped. But I think the difference in 1972 lay in the canvassers; last year's crusaders seemed joyless, humorless. A high school junior stuffing envelopes at campaign headquarters told me that when she was young—what is she now?—she was a socialist. Another group of students left, after an hour of knocking on doors, to go snowmobiling. Somebody else, getting on the bus for home, said, "This makes the fifth weekend I've worked for the campaign," and I was suddenly struck by the fact that we'd all been compiling similar figures—how many miles we'd walked, how many houses we'd visited. In 1968 we believed, and so we shivered; in 1972, we shivered so that we might believe. Our candidate was perhaps no less believable, but our idealism had soured and our motives had become less noble. We went to Berlin—many of us—so we could say "I canvassed in New Hampshire," the way high school kids join clubs so they can write "I'm a member of the Latin Club" on their college applications. The students for McGovern whom I worked with were engaged in a business deal, trading frost-bitten fingers for guilt-free consciences. Nineteen sixty-eight's dreams and abstractions just didn't hold up on a bill of sale.

President Nixon announced the mining of Haiphong harbor in the spring of my freshman year at Yale. I waited to feel again the outrage I'd experienced three years before when our Armed Forces invaded first Cambodia and then Kent State, but I stayed numb. It was as though each new Vietnam development and each unfruitful protest raised our threshold of tolerance—mine, at least—as if, like insects growing used to DDT, we'd built up an immunity, an indifference. Or—and this is a sadder commentary on ourselves than on the government—that few people can maintain, indefinitely, enthusiasm for a cause that doesn't affect them personally. The draft no longer threatened so much, and opposition to the war was no longer so fashionably radical. For whatever reason, in any case, there was little protest. A few students behaved responsively, of course—talking low, crying even, not eating much. It seemed faintly immoral to eat, wrong to care, still, about food when villages were being destroyed and civilians dying. But I confess my discomfort came not because I was upset but because I felt I ought to be.

Outside my window there were marchers, chanters, rallies, bed sheet banners with messages (SCREW NIXON). There was no single big group, though; instead, a dozen

straggly and uncompelling ones, like groups of wandering
Christmas carolers in March. Bad enough that the redun-
dancy of this doubtful outcry had weakened it. More than
that, it weakened in retrospect the really forceful and well
executed statements made back in the sixties. Better to
have stayed inside, maybe, and left to the imagination how
many people cared. We would have pictured grander
crowds.

I am suspicious-natured. I look for the lowest motives,
aware of what they are as only one who feels them herself
can be aware. So when I saw the Haiphong demonstrators, reruns of 1969, it seemed to me (because that's what
my motives might have been) that what they were involved in was nostalgia—lots of "remember how it was in
Washington? . . . the flowers in the National Guardsmen's
guns, the candlelight, the dead soldiers' names, handcuffs
locked to the White House gate . . ." It was an attempt to
perform again a gesture that can have real impact only
once. (To kill a man in self-defense takes just one well-
aimed bullet. Firing again and again alters the spirit of the
act.) Those straggly April marches, the petitions and demands for strikes, seemed only to remind us all of how
the last great demonstrations, May Day 1969 and the
November moratorium, had failed to bring about a
change. Now they seemed founded not in disappointment
that the country had failed to do the good things we
hoped it would, but based, instead, on bitterness—there
was an I-told-you-so-ish feeling surrounding what was
going on, as if the actions of that spring only confirmed
what we'd expected all along—the worst. Demonstrators
on the lookout for injustice and brutality found it, of
course, responding with a cry of "Pigs" and before the
provocation had even come, like too-well-rehearsed actors
who give their lines before they get their cues. New Haven
atrocities were traded like baseball cards and marbles
("How many times did they hit you?" "Well, *I* got arrest-
ed . . .") while Vietnam, it seemed to me, got mentioned
very little. It was a time for vanity and demagoguery and
political power struggles and legitimized cowboys and In-
dians, and I didn't like it, most of all because it put in an
unfair light the people who were genuinely and, still rarer,
selflessly distressed about the war.

Girls of my generation (I should call them women, I know, but old, pre-liberation habits linger on) are often asked for their opinions on Women's Lib (the abbreviation is, in itself, the beginning of a diminution of the cause), and one predictable answer, read off with a seemly giggle, is that every girl likes to have doors opened for her on dates. Or she can launch into a Rights of Women talk about the prostitution of marriage and the chauvinism of the media.

Most likely, though, she'll nervously, cautiously seat herself on the fence, legs crossed demurely at the ankle, chin out to show she is no southern belle, and torn between the desire to save her cake and the desire to eat it now, she'll say that yes, she's all for equal rights and equal pay, and day care centers are fine for some people, and TV commercials—though they certainly don't influence *her*—are a disgrace, but she doesn't care for the movement's *style*—those women are too loud and coarse, they come on too strong, they have no sense of humor, they intimidate and antagonize the very people they're trying to convert—other women. She doesn't like the bitterness she sees so often among feminists. (Why is it that, like nuns, they're often so plain? Sour grapes, she'll say.) She *likes* men. She *wants* to get married and have children—she's for (the old cliché) *human* liberation.

It's an easy out, that line—incontestable. Is anyone in favor of unequal jobs and unequal pay? Feminists would regard the fence sitter as a sellout and a traitor, and I guess they'd see me that way too. Because, while I'm conscious of the cliché, that is—to a great extent—how I feel. I do not feel inferior or unliberated, and while I recognize that there are women who do, women (for whom the movement does a great service) whose image of themselves needs to be changed, and that even those of us who *feel* equal to men may not get equal treatment, the truth is that the methods of the feminist movement turn me off. Sexist that, in some ways, I might be called, I think first of looks, and am aware of what it is about Germaine Greer and Gloria Steinem that appeals to me. Almost certainly they would reject the idea that their function is to give the movement glamour, but much of their importance to the movement comes, unquestionably, from the slim, stylish, graceful-moving image they project. (Gloria Steinem can liberate as only someone on the other side of prison bars can unlock a door.) Women who are attracted to her use the same set of standards I use, when I find myself unattracted to them—they like her looks as I dislike theirs; they want to be associated with her style and poise as I want to disassociate myself from their stylelessness— from women too old to go blue-jeaned and braless, from the tousled haired and the tensely scrawny and the ones whose eyes bear the look of frustration and anger that have more than memories of unfair pay behind them. Women with "Vaginal Politics" buttons pinned to the zippers on their jeans; women who call me *sister,* who speak, in locker-room, army-barracks lingo of being "fucked over by the crappy shit" men hand them. I feel my privacy intruded upon with orgasm and sex-object talk.

The actions of large groups, when they assemble, frighten me a bit. United we stand, divided we fall—I know that. But the effects crowds have on the people in them are often dangerous and deceptive. When individuals join in affection and good feeling (as at a folk music concert) the atmosphere of warmth (while it may be illusory and deceptive) seems healthy. But people in crowds stir each other up to a point where good sense is suspended by too much strong feeling in too-close quarters, too much chanting and foot-stomping and hand-clapping. I think of the football game I went to once, where the wild, touchdown-crazed crowds made the wooden stands we sat on creak and then crumble. Films of Hitler in action, of the Rolling Stones at Altamont—the analogies I make are rash and perhaps unfair to a movement that unquestionably does good. But it is, nonetheless, a movement held together by shared negative feeling, a sisterhood of bitterness and sometimes hate.

I grew up wanting to have babies. I reject what would be the feminist attitude that TV and baby dolls and the male-dominated American culture brainwashed me. I *did* play with baby dolls and watch TV (and am appalled now, watching old reruns, to see the notions of A Woman's Place they uniformly presented), but it wasn't those things that gave me my dreams of motherhood, and what sexist notions they exposed me to I think I rejected.

(Desi's tyranny over Lucy, and her sly wheedling always seemed—more than anything else—dumb.) I wanted to have children (and, if I'd been a boy, I'd have felt the same way) not because I had a low opinion of myself and considered myself good for nothing else or because my own mother presented an oppressed housewife image in our family (which she never did) but just because I like kids.

But something new seems to be happening. Friends of mine announce now that they don't intend to marry or that, if they do, they won't have children. Often they are children of divorced parents or parents who, they tell me casually, don't like each other much. It all seems strange and sad and unromantic, this lack of faith in families and permanence, the short-attention-span notion of finding life-long companionship a bore and any kind of ties and restrictions a slur on that sixties ideal we grew up with, that what mattered more than anything else was *freedom*. It was a time when discipline and even simple regimen seemed unfashionable. When we wrote at school, we were encouraged to forget about grammar and concern our-selves with free self-expression—maybe not to write at all, but instead to nonverbally communicate.

At home we were not spanked or given heavy chores, most of us. And by some obscure route I think all that has brought us around to doubts about families and order in general. We are suspicious of anything that seems too rigid, anything that seems to endanger the carefree, don't-think-ahead life. It has been said, and it's true, that the future seems too uncertain for us to make plans, that the specter of The Bomb and ecological disaster hangs over us. The feeling many of us have about marriage and children comes from a kind of Peter Pan feeling about Youth—a stage of life so glamorized in our time that we no longer eagerly anticipate being grown-ups (as teen-agers used to, when growing up meant escaping the strict rule of parents). Now it is Youth, not adults, who wield the power. Getting married and having children means that, if you are not old, at least you are no longer young.

THE WORDS *ambitious, up-and-coming, go-getting* used to be the highest compliment awarded to a bright young man just starting out on his career. Back in those days, the label *businessman* held no unfortunate connotations, no ring of war-mongering or conservatism or pollution. The future may have been uncertain, but it was certainly considered, anyway, and the goals were clear: a good marriage, a good job, a good income—that was a good life.

My generation's definition of The Good Life is harder to arrive at. Our plans for the future are vague, because so many of us don't believe in planning, because we don't quite believe in the future. Perhaps we make too much of growing up with tension, from as far back as the Cuban Missile Crisis, but the fact is that the tension of the sixties put us in a kind of suspension. There were always fallout shelter signs, always secret servicemen and always, when the words "we interrupt this program to bring you ..." flashed on the screen, the possibility of an assassination. When a plane flies low I wonder (just for a second)—is it the Russians? The Chinese?

So we don't plan. We make a thing of spontaneity and informality. (Parties just *happen*; couples hang around together—no more going on dates.) Looking ahead to the future, planning, and pushing are seen as uncool ("take it easy . . . no sweat"), aggressive.

It's impossible not to wonder where the young hip kids of today will be twenty years from now. Their parents say they'll settle down ("We were wild in our day too . . .") and some of them will—some will later join their parents' establishment world just as, for now, they've joined a group that is itself a kind of establishment. But there's another group, involved in much more than a fad, and their futures are less easy to predict. They've passed beyond faddishness, beyond the extreme activism of the late sixties and arrived at a calm isolationist position—free not just from the old establishment ambitions and the corporate tycoon style, but from the aggressiveness of the radical tycoon. The best thing to be, for them isn't go-getting or up-and-coming, but cool. Broad social conscience has been replaced by personal responsibility, and if they plan at all, their plans will be to get away. The new movement is away from the old group forms of moratorium crowds and huge rock concerts and communes. Young doctors who once joined the Peace Corps are turning more and more to small-town private practices, Harvard scholars are dropping out to study auto mechanics or farming. Everybody wants to buy land in Oregon and Vermont. If we have any ambition at all now, it is not so much the drive to get ahead as it is the drive to get away.

When my friends and I were little, we had big plans. I would be a famous actress and singer, dancing on the side. I would paint my own sets and compose my own music, writing the script and the lyrics and reviewing the performance for the New York *Times*. I would marry and have three children (they don't allow us dreams like that any more) and we would live, rich and famous, (donating lots to charity, of course, and periodically adopting orphans), in a house we designed ourselves. When I was older I had visions of good works. I saw myself in South American rain forests and African deserts, feeding the hungry and healing the sick with an obsessive selflessness,

I see now, that was as selfish, in the end, as my first plans for stardom.

Now my goal is simpler. I want to be happy. And I want comfort—nice clothes, a nice house, good music and good food, and the feeling that I'm doing some little thing that matters. I'll vote and I'll give to charity, but I won't give myself. I feel a sudden desire to buy land—not a lot, not as a business investment, but just a small plot of earth so that whatever they do to the country I'll have a place where I can go—a kind of fallout shelter, I guess. As some people prepare for their old age, so I prepare for my twenties. A little house, a comfortable chair, peace and quiet—retirement sounds tempting.

I'm almost twenty now—two decades gone. I know now that I will never be a ballerina. That's not because of any conscious choice, because of anything I've done, but because of what's been neglected. It isn't that I ever longed to be one, but the knowledge scares me, that I can't—there's nothing, absolutely nothing I can do about it. I am too old to be a violin prodigy, or to learn championship chess; I'm closer to Ophelia now than Juliet. The word *woman* embarrasses me a little. (Why is that? Some left-over scrap of unliberation, that *boys are men*, while I remain, and will till I am fifty, always a *girl*.)

Once, I guess, youth was a handicap and coming of age an exciting, horizon-broadening time for long pants and freedom. For us, today, youth—while it lasts—is a time we greedily hold onto, a fashionable, glorified age when, if we don't quite *swing*, at least we're told that's what we do, that these are the best years of our lives—it's all downhill from here.

But I'm basically an optimist. Somehow, no matter what the latest population figures say, I feel everything will work out—just like on TV. I may doubt man's fundamental goodness, but I believe in his power to survive. I say, sometimes, that I wonder if we'll be around in thirty years, but then I forget myself and speak of "when I'm fifty. . . ." Death has touched me now—from Vietnam and Biafra and a car accident that makes me buckle my seat belt—but like negative numbers and the sound of a dog whistle (too high-pitched for human ears), it's not a concept I can comprehend.

1973

It is the new year now. (I rang it in with popcorn and Guy Lombardo, sad to see that even the seemingly ageless Royal Canadians had compromised to sound contemporary, *with-it*.) I'm sitting by a window in New Hampshire—I have left Yale, Chaucer classes and dormitory bunk beds for the mountains—watching the evening grosbeaks crowded at the bird feeder. They are ugly-natured birds who scare away the chickadees, but nice to look at, fighting over sunflower seeds and suet, winging away at the least sound or movement from me in my chair. The wind is strong right now—just about sunset; the temperature reads eight degrees below zero. In here, though, I am warm. The fire is laid, although not burning (old *TV Guides*, this morning's New York *Times* and dripping, snowy logs), the dog wheezes in a back room (old and asthmatic, he hibernates in winter, dreaming of a badger-hunting spring) and a tangerine peel, filled up with seeds, sits on the table next to me. The television set is off—nothing but golf tournaments and football games this Sunday afternoon—so I have played Monopoly, putting hotels on every property I owned, and won. The winning matters still. I count my paper money like a miser, rejoice beyond all reasonable proportions when I take in another hundred. I'm thinking what I'll have for dinner, scribbling in the margins of my yellow legal pad, examining the split ends of my hair, watching the sky change colors, checking my watch, the *TV Guide,* the temperature again. The bird feeder is empty now.

I have just finished reading my manuscript. I've come out here, to this chair, this window, with this yellow pad, to write the ending to this book. Before me is a list of topics to tie up in some fine and final-sounding paragraph. Now is the moment, maybe, to quickly, deftly plug in gaps—things about my parents that should be here and aren't, about my best friend, next-door neighbor Becky, my one real high school boy friend, the year at Exeter I barely mention. I should perhaps temper my statements with apologies, for saying "we" all through this book, when there are so many people I've no right to speak for (where are the blacks? the teen-age dropouts? the people of my generation who read—really read—books? I cannot speak for them). I need an ending, something that will tie in air-raid drills and Dr. Kildare shows and fifth-grade facts-of-life talks and college board tests and debutante balls, some statement that will make my scattered thoughts seem pointed all in one direction, toward a single, nineteen-sixties summing-up conclusion, some idea that will conceal the fact that when I wrote this book I had no notion of what all the pieces would add up to. But any generalization I make now would be more than a bit contrived because, like yearbooks and Sears catalogues, one's memories rarely have shape and form and (high school English) Main Ideas. Ten years can't be summed up; a generation can't be generalized about.

So I'll say one more thing, just for myself, about the dog and the red-breasted nuthatch and the chickadees and even the grosbeaks, also the home-grown summer squash and peas I'm about to thaw from the freezer for dinner, and the fields where, last August, I picked them. The plants and animals are the telling omissions in my recollections of the decade—too many passing fads, too little that is lasting. I will resist my debater's instinct to end with a ringing phrase. It's suppertime.

AVON 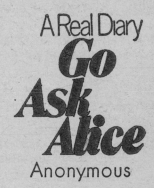 NEW LEADER
IN PAPERBACKS

A Real Diary

Go
Ask
Alice

Anonymous

N431   95¢

A young girl's story of her tragic experiences with drugs.

"An extraordinary work for teenagers . . . A superior work . . . A document of horrifying reality . . . It's the kind of work we wish our kids would take to heart." *The New York Times*

THE BIG BESTSELLERS
ARE AVON BOOKS!

The Wolf and the Dove
Kathleen E. Woodiwiss   18457 $1.75

The Golden Soak
Hammond Innes   18465 $1.50

The Priest
Ralph McInerny   18192 $1.75

Emerald Station
Daoma Winston   18200 $1.50

Sweet Savage Love
Rosemary Rogers   17988 $1.75

How I Found Freedom
In An Unfree World
Harry Browne   17772 $1.95

I'm OK—You're OK
Thomas A. Harris, M.D.   14662 $1.95

Jonathan Livingston Seagull
Richard Bach   14316 $1.50

Open Marriage
George and Nena O'Neill   14084 $1.95

You & I
Leonard Nimoy   17616 $1.50

Maria
Maria Von Trapp   17921 $1.50

The Divorce
Stephen Longstreet   17244 $1.50

Nothing By Chance
Richard Bach   14704 $1.50

Where better paperbacks are sold, or directly from the publisher. Include 15¢ per copy for mailing; allow three weeks for delivery.

Avon Books, Mail Order Dept., 250 West 55th Street, New York, N. Y. 10019